Choice Words

Books by Randy Blasing

Light Years
To Continue
The Particles
The Double House of Life
Graphic Scenes
Second Home

TRANSLATIONS (WITH MUTLU KONUK):

Poems of Nazim Hikmet
Nazim Hikmet: Human Landscapes from My Country

Choice Words

Poems 1970–2005

Randy Blasing

Copper Beech Press
Providence

Grateful acknowledgment is made to the editors of the magazines that first published some of the newer poems here: *Michigan Quarterly Review* ("Who Shall Remain Nameless," "Creature Feature"), *Poetry* ("Byzantine Bird"), and *The Southern Review* ("Arrhythmia"). The older poems originally appeared—often in different form and sometimes under different titles—in *The Carolina Quarterly, The Literary Review, Michigan Quarterly Review, Modern Poetry Studies, The Nation, The New Criterion, The Paris Review, Persea, Poet & Critic, Poetry, Poetry Now, The Sewanee Review, The Southern Review, Southwest Review, The Virginia Quarterly Review, Western Humanities Review,* and *The Yale Review;* in *For the Birds* (Turkey Press, 1975), a limited edition; and in *Light Years* (Persea, 1977), *To Continue* (Persea, 1983), *The Particles* (Copper Beech, 1983), *The Double House of Life* (Persea, 1989), *Graphic Scenes* (Persea, 1994), and *Second Home* (Copper Beech, 2001).

"Cardiogram," "Byzantine Bird," and "Refuge" were reprinted in *Articulations* (University of Iowa), *And We the Creatures* (Dream Horse Press), and *The POETRY Anthology, 1912-2002* (Ivan R. Dee).

Library of Congress Cataloguing-in-Publication Data

Blasing, Randy.
    Choice words : poems, 1970–2005 / Randy Blasing.—1st ed.
        p. cm.
    ISBN 0-914278-82-7 (pbk. : alk. paper)
    I. Title.

PS3552.L38C48   2007
811'.54—dc22   2006049249

ISBN-13: 978-0-914278-82-5

Set in Bembo by Sans Serif
Printed and bound by McNaughton & Gunn
Manufactured in the United States of America
First Edition

for Charles Sullivan

Find in middle air
An eagle on the wing,
Recognise the five
That make the Muses sing.
                    W. B. Yeats

CONTENTS

NEW POEMS *(2005)*

from LIGHT YEARS *(1977)*

THE WORLD IN MINIATURE

The earth has you in the diminutive
to thank who gave rise to a minute young
tender orange shoot you coaxed from seed

& watched—its husk sloughed off—branch out at last
to flower tautly in what little light
the papery March sky admits to it

this skinflint morning dimmed with snow, as though
the day had broken in a thousand places
into a million such pinpoint white blossoms.

NORTH OF AMHERST

(Mohawk Trail, 1972)

A river more rocks than water
sidled up to a road jays set
blue explosions off all along.
Hills surfaced in the distance, filled
with orange trees the wind defoliated,
& in the threatening sky the sun
got snuffed. The trail lost, my friends gone
up in smoke with the war, Deerfield Village
sneaked up on me after the massacre
of 1704.
             The streets
were empty & the place was dead. I peeked
inside the houses, found no sign of life,
& walked until at length I stood
upon the grounds of its academy
like some burnt graduate who could
still hear, however faintly, cries that drifted
back to the now-deserted school
one dark Saturday toward the bitter
end of another perfect fall.

HOG HEAVEN

Gobs of clouds foam
up around the edges;
the sky lies buried
in the swimming pool.

Nature & everything
—evergreen oaks, a lake, the boat
upon it & the man in *it*—
all lead their still lives.

Two things I've never understood:
electricity & the Holy Ghost.
The water glitters
with lots of tiny plus & minus signs.

Poolside, an ink-spotted rust butterfly
flexes its wings, catching the light.

ALL PRESENT

The sky is
blue irises
verging on
lilacs. The so-
called evening
star has six
—no, five ("count
'em")—points. There
are stars you
didn't see,

you think. Wrong
again—they weren't
there before. It's
that time of day
or night, which kind
of thrills you: stars
are popping
up across
the sky this
instant. Change

raises time
to the power
of *now*—no
before or
after! Such
moments let
you in on
the secret
of being:
becoming.

ON WATER

Sometimes, you say, the sea
is rocky, with jagged
edges like quartz, other
times it's plowed in even

rows like a field of blue
earth, & some days it grows
so still & flat that you
can't tell where the water

ends & the air starts. Or
there are days (& nights) when
the sea gives off white sparks,
its fire fanned by the wind.

But stare at the sea blankly
—for days on end—& soon
the sea itself is all
a blank. It's like a common

word you keep repeating
to yourself until it
sounds so strange that the thing
it names no longer is.

PASSAGES

1. Izmir

A minor earthquake just shook me awake—
a city built on an underground cave!
Breakfast is green plums, white cheese, & black honey.

2. Hotel Kismet

Spread-eagled on a rock in the sun
by the sea, I take myself
seriously—a beached starfish!
A *bleached* starfish: I point in five
directions, like our conception
of a star.

Here we all are, living it up
royally while swimming under the shadow
of six Turkish gunboats at bay.
Suddenly I have the feeling I'm back
in the Balkans, watching the First
World War get underway
sixty summers late.

I see, across the bay, the square stone faces
of white village houses dotted with windows
& thrown together on the hill like dice.

A perfect halo of stars overhead
flies to pieces as the stars circulate
through the night.

In town I'm everyone I see:
I'm German &, I'm proud to say, from Hamburg,
or I'm a Turkish sailor on my way
back to my ship & maybe to a war

on Cyprus, my face as round & smooth
& worried-looking as the striped
watermelon in my arms.

The white line of the horizon, meeting ground
of sea, sky, & Greek island in the hazy
distance, burns like a fuse.

The icy honey of a Tuborg beer
fills my glass. I raise it & drink
to the sun.

3. Bodrum

Lightning-white houses ground a spark-blue sky
here in the land of dark bread & honey.

Cherries, apricots, plums, peaches, grapes, pears—
the fruits of the earth grow on trees
& fall into our hands
one after another,
as if dropped from heaven
on earth.

I walk through their museum of a castle
in sandals much the same as those they wore
ten centuries ago. I'm looking at
some cups & dishes from prehistory—
people survived by their eating utensils!
How will I ever face my plate
staring me in the face three times a day
for the rest of my days? Today, however,
my feet are killing me, so here
I stand, worrying about fallen arches.

This morning I awoke to martial music
in the streets, fighting on Cyprus
between Greece & Turkey.

All day I have to keep
reminding myself there's a war too close
for comfort.

Tonight there's a blackout
on purpose. We've been asked
to "blue" our lights, which means masking them
with a cross between blue tissue paper
& wax paper. Schoolchildren use the stuff
for book covers.

Watching the sky above
the blacked-out town
is like looking down from a jet descending
on a city of stars.

Now I see what's milky
about the Milky Way.

They woke the whole town before it was light:
"Our spies in Athens expect an air raid
at dawn!" I ran
for the foothills, the jets minutes away
on Cos, & found a hole
I crawled into, eyeing as a helmet
one rusty bucket. That's how scared
I was, & am.

When news comes on the radio, people
grow quiet & bow their heads
in concentration, as if to pray.

The black, after-dinner sky is clotted
with creamy stars.

If only I could take Thoreau's comfort
in staring down the Milky Way
& repeating the words "*our* galaxy"
(my italics).

This morning a Voice of America
bulletin announced a cease-fire on Cyprus.

4. Didyma

Floating on my back in the sea,
I get all turned around, a compass needle
searching for north.

The sea refuses to show its true colors.
It goes from green to violet
via aquamarine & royal blue
& back again by way of maroon, pales
at sundown to a milky white with streaks
of lavender or pink, then stretches out
flat on its back to sleep. At night it tosses
in its sleep, & mine. Daylight brings it peace,
until it wakes with a glazed look
to the wind rising with the rising sun.

I can just see you waving
up from the beach at me
above it. Even
the medium-size people
dwarf you, you small
person turning your back
on the shifty sea. Then

you go into your almost military,
Miss America walk—what a commotion!

An old man who was retired from the army,
& whose son also had retired
from the service, dropped dead this afternoon
on his way down the beach to go swimming.
While three soldiers stood around his body,
his son came up & lay down at his side
on the sand, there on the beach where his father fell.

I make a wish at the drop of a star.
My thirtieth year ends here.

5. *Istanbul*

It was hardly the middle
of August, pomegranates
still blushing unplucked
in the leaves, but already
the sun had visibly
weakened, falling for autumn. Now
at the end, I sing
the praises of red-
faced tomatoes about
to burst, cheeky yellow peaches
splotched crimson, roly-poly
pears, mustard melons summer
swelled up so sweetly
they burn, honeycombs of golden
green grapes, the caviar
of black, plus glossy
deep-purple eggplants the light
shines the color of night.

from TO CONTINUE *(1983)*

BLUR

the sun blisters
the snowy fields with lakes

it's still early
February but the wind is

pure March
I'd know its big sloppy kisses

of air anywhere
I know this feeling

in my stomach
something between hunger

& excitement not quite
butterflies but more like

what happens when I see
green eyes

1. Providence

I tear myself away from the Atlantic
at sunup & head out
of the east into the blaze of days,
the lion of light breathing down my neck.

2. Purple Heart Highway

I see things through a silver haze
of heat.

The air is hot
as blood.

3. I-90 (Mass Pike)

Blue hills bubble the horizon
as I go west at last.

The quicksilver Connecticut
freezes in time.

4. I-90 (NY Thruway)

Late in the day I catch
the Hudson going to its death below.

The light stops & glances over its shoulder,
leaving the earth.

The sky looks bruised
where the sun was.

The Mohawk stalks
the straggler day into the dark.

Tonight the new moon starts
carving a place for itself in the sky.

5. *Dream Lodge*

I crawl into the cave of sleep & take
refuge in dreams.

6. *Finger Lakes*

"Take your boy to see the Mets yet?" a town
father at the counter of the Country
Bumpkin Diner asks the young guy sitting
next to him. But the guy answers
with silence, so he wonders: "Don't you have
a boy?" "I lost him five years ago;
got only girls now." My eyes fall
on the cutting edges
of the stainless-steel cream pitcher
in front of me. I look back up,
& the guy is long gone.

7. *Niagara Falls*

Jade-green water
barreling over the Falls breaks
into a cascade of smashed headlight glass.

The poor souls getting on the boat
down below disappear
in black for their journey into the mist.

8. I-75

The last summer my father saw, he taught me
how to stay alive on the road, driving
this now-deserted highway up
into Michigan on our way back home
to Minnesota. *Never drop
below eighty-five,* he'd go, *watch
the mirror for cops, & don't start passing
until you're sitting right
on the guy's tail.* In the back seat
my mother would turn white when he'd say
to gun it in the face
of an onrushing car, all 365
horses of the '63 Dodge
breaking loose at once.

9. US 2

Sun about gone, fish turn up dead
on the rocks of Lake Michigan.

Just after dawn I look into the woods:
night is hiding out in the trees.

10. US 8

I pop an Olympia on the shore
of Crescent Lake in Wisconsin & drink
to its lasting good health.

I drink in the *café-au-lait* St. Croix.
How could I have missed
the Mississippi?

11. *Minneapolis*

I walk into another death: my mother's
mother just shipwrecked here
94 years, 10 months, & 13 days
out of Bergen, Norway.

12. *US 169*

Down in the Valley of the Jolly Green
Giant, I pass the Minnesota River
& stumble on the town
of Henderson ("Pop. 760") where
my father grew up. It's a Saturday
morning, & along comes
the sheriff in his black
squad car to check me out. He then
proceeds to park himself
across the street & keep an eye
on my progress
down it. Instead, I cross him up by walking
over & asking him who knows
where my father lived. He
does, & points to a brick house I can't see
for the trees. He even
lets me in on my grandfather's strange passion
for eels. The name *Blasing* is still written
in stone on what was once
his drugstore but is now
the Legion Bar, a red-&-yellow sign
for Grain Belt Beer outside. The three kids hanging
around the corner turn
out to be Indians, the only life
in sight.

13. I-90

South Dakota, & the country
falls flat.

The gunsmoke-blue
Missouri: a surprise
oasis!

Across the river, sun scuffs green hills brown.

Rolling hills breaking up
into planes of yellow, green, & black drop
away on all
sides, expanding my horizon
until I'm circled by the sky.

This testing the limits
of space creates
a vacuum in my head.

14. Motel West

When I pull in,
a beat white Impala is parked
outside the door
next to ours. Stuff is piled up to
& on top of
the roof of the car. It happens the guy
comes out & gathers we're not much
better off ourselves, so he asks us to start
drinking with him
& his lady. He left his wife
in Iowa, she her husband, & both
their jobs. Maybe they'll end

up in Reno & stay
with his aunt. He made the cooler
where he stashes his Pabst
himself. Over the roar
of a semi idling out on the side
of the road, he tells us how his good friend
OD'd at last after years of nightmares
about the war. Dusk falls
like a fine dust
settling. Strangers, we keep
on smiling as we talk,
the summer night rising around our ankles.
We wish us luck.

15. Badlands

I step into the future here & now,
walking among the ruins of the earth.

16. Black Hills

Rapid City shoots me twenty-five years
into the past to getting shaken out
of sleep & run out of town in the dark,
minutes ahead of a big flash flood.

17. US 85

This rainy Sunday
I shudder through lonesome
Wyoming toward sundown, so much nothing
burning a hole
in my empty stomach
like bad coffee.

18. Continental Divide

The stone-
faced Rockies cut
into the air & leave us all
gasping.

19. Boulder

Today launches me on my thirty-fifth year
as I wake up
high outside of Denver, caught in the middle
of America, hung up between two oceans.

20. I-25

Blue mesas & low, sombrero-like green
mountains: it's suddenly
New Mexico, & I can breathe again.

21. US 64

Horse, I can see
standing in that yellow meadow,
nose buried in the book
of wildflowers!

22. Taos

This afternoon
a mushroom cloud towers

over the Blood of Christ Mountains
back of Taos.

The sun sets orange-on-yellow, as on
the license plates of all the pickups here.

The gorge outside town dry-gulches
the meandering Rio Grande.

23. Taos Pueblo

Sky cruel. Always
scraping roof
of pueblo. No
ladder enough.
Doors & window
frames same bad
blue. Legs now,
too. The false sky
turquoise, & their eyes.

24. Taos Highway

The sun just making it over the mountains
yellow-bricks the Santa Fe road.

I pass on
Los Alamos.

Tan Santa Fe wakes up
all rosy, an island of light
buoyed by air.

25. I-40

A smoke signal
of a cloud spirals out
of the hills past

Albuquerque, the code
unbroken still.

26. *Gallup*

Big rigs looming out of the Sunkist west,
a massive lavender cloud trailing rain
off to the north, & the Santa Fe freight:
boxcars stampeding into the night.

27. *US 666*

Window Rock, Sky
City: the Zunis lie
behind me, dead
south.

28. *Ruins Road*

Atomic Signs
Orbit Car Wash
Dizzy Land Liquors
Starlite Bowling

29. *Aztec*

"The Pueblo Indian considers everything around him—the
plants, rocks and animals, the sky, earth & clouds—his
equal. All are alive & each has a personality. He is one of a
highly formalized, ritualized group who, through prayers &
chants, seeks to keep all things living together in harmony."

30. *Mesa Verde*

No lights below, & closer than ever to the stars
while still on earth.

Moon, you're so full of yourself you don't know
tomorrow the night will begin
chipping away at you.

Here in the presence of the Anasazi,
their cliff-side condominiums
bring me the peace
of places where people have lived,
buried their dead, & disappeared.

I get to know
rabbitbrush, lupine, gold weed, Indian
paintbrush, scarlet bugler, & tansy aster.

Dumb hummingbird hovers
around my Coors.

Turquoise dreams
two nights running . . .

31. Navajo Trail

Sallow ground breaks
out in blotches
a sickly green.

Arizona
reddens.

Land so bad I
can't figure why
on earth anyone
would fence
it in is
nothing but
a reservation.

"You Are Now Leaving the Ute Indian Reservation.
We Hope You Have Enjoyed the Scenery."

32. Grand Canyon

Sitting here at the edge
of the Canyon, watching a blue
cloud block my view
of the sunset, I feel the pull of earth
two billion years away.

The side-winding Colorado snakes down
through the ages
of rock in the distance.
Unmoving to the naked eye, it races
headlong toward its dream of the sea.

33. US 66

Blood oozes from the ground
—even rocks bleed—as I descend
into Nevada, rushing west for gold.

. . . & you, like love, guiding me down
the red roads, the main arteries
of this country, seeking the heart.

34. Las Vegas

Hope abandoned
for chance, all-night neon
bushwhacks Orion & Cassiopeia
out here where the stars go to die.

35. I-15

The air thickens to a pink haze
above the Mojave
as I barrel down the gun-gray freeway
toward L.A.

Suddenly the sky
is missing:
it's burned
to the ground.

36. The Basin

I plug the TV in & switch
it on, a face
swims up to the surface
without a sound.

I tune into the dream
& call it home
here as the sun breaks down
in the Pacific, another day junked.

NIGHT MUSIC

Full moon spotlights the yard, two chairs
& a table empty
as they naturally are, you & I gone
as we must be . . .

I can hear the camellia bush stir
itself in the shadows,
the innumerable tiny pink petals
spiraling out of the hard buds to be there
in the morning, surprising me
like the first stars
when I pull back the leaves
& discover them underneath, blushing . . .

This is the moon
that lays me bare in X-ray light,
this is day seen
against the background of what waits ahead . . .

It's the blackbird in the lemon tree, not the tree
alone, yellow with lemons, that I love,
not mountains diamond-backed with snow alone
but blackening in the sun, rising out
of the earth like stored-up darkness,
not noon alone,
beast-sleepy, but the cat's eyes widening
at evening to take in the night.

SONORA WILDFLOWERS

All kinds pressed in a book no one can read
until the life is squeezed
out of them. Then
when you open to the pages
where they are, you find their million colors
gone, & flattened
they don't look anything like you remember,
your memory of them alive
erased by seeing them
this way—object lessons
in solid geometry, where the missing
dimension of depth gets left to the old
imagination, which never could fathom
busying your head with fleshing out cones,
cylinders, & spheres. It's the same as when
the inevitable black camera shoots
to kill, freezing you as you were,
& the photograph takes
off on its own, wearing your smile
wherever it goes, no
souvenir of you but something that stands
in your stead, i.e., instead of the figure
caught posing as you, you who are dropping
out of the picture at the speed of light,
the big picture, which you illuminate
with the flare of a match struck in the dark
the way stars do the night,
falling. Tomorrow already
filling with smoke & burning down
around you now, you'd panic if it weren't
for a walk in the shadow-swept spring desert
teaching you still is how to be.

COAST TO COAST

1. Memorial Day in the Golden State

I no sooner named the jacarandas here
than they blossomed into a Milton Avery—
blue trees! The pink-satin roses have gone
to pieces, ditto the black-hearted scarlets.
Downy fruit studs the apricots, green thumbs
of hummingbirds nose around in the last
of the bottle-brushes. What does anyone
remember? Suddenly the sky goes grainy
with stars, & my eyes crisscross the abyss
it is in the end: Orion's
Belt an ellipsis, the Big Dipper coming
up empty. I stand on the edge
of summer as on the verge of a promise
made to be broken.

2. Independence Day in the Ocean State

The dead wave their little flags from their yard
as I cruise past
bruise-colored hydrangeas
to the beach. Picnickers in clumps
of two or three
wrap up in blankets, feeling clouds
muscle in on the sun. Far out
on the pewter water, sails flare
like candles on a birthday cake. I follow
the blacktop shadowing the all-rock shore,
& a small plane floats a message
from my local travel agent:
Escape. Rain scatters everyone,
no-see-ums eating me alive.

from THE PARTICLES *(1983)*

OVER DRINKS

Drink, drank, drunk, Roman
Jakobson says, retreat
into the past, i.e.,

their respective
vowels originate
progressively farther back

in the mouth. *Yes,* I'm quick
to acknowledge, *the present is always
on the tip of my tongue.*

RAMAZAN AT NEW PHOCAEA

Today the children, rich & poor alike,
have been reborn, glowing from head to toe

in new clothes. The three little girls I saw
riding here in a blue pickup this morning

under their father's watchful eyes looked fresh
as daisies, their sun-browned faces haloed

by identical straw-blond summer hats,
& now the three sisters materialize

on the scorched beach like figments of the heat,
promenading in white holiday dresses

polka dots sprinkle all the colors
of raindrops in the sun. They go to show

everyone is created in the image
of light, & every last day is holy.

GILGAMESH VISITS EPHESUS

My skin drinks in the white poison
of the sun. The stone remains of the great

city blacken in the dead air
of August. Headless columns giving rise

to nothing but the sky make their points
bluntly, & recently the library

has been rebuilt to look
bombed-out. I see into the past

of the future: daily life is history.
The cicadas stammer insistently.

These perfect hand-cut stones
have something to tell me, holding their peace.

THE PARTICLES

How I shot up
at the speed of light, sun
in my veins & the moon
in my bones! At ten
I'd wake up early
& go crouch in the den
in the gloom before school,
not to miss the latest
test on TV. It was always daybreak
in the desert, & I witnessed
the fate of dummy nuclear families
seated at breakfast various distances
from ground zero. Our flaming red
house faced east & looked out
across a valley that caught fire
every autumn. I remember my father
pointing to the city, three miles
off where the sun
came from, & saying someday *it* would happen
there, dawning on us "in a white-
hot flash." In all
those years I only saw one dawn,
when a bunch of us stood on our green hill
& took the chance of a lifetime to see
the sun eclipsed.
Squinting through bits
of exposed film
or slivers of smoked glass,
we shivered together
in the summer morning
when darkness fell as the sun rose,
as if out of the blue
a black umbrella had opened
over our heads. I broke down at eleven
& threw a tantrum over grammar, lost

among the parts
of speech. But I stayed after school
with blond Mrs. Johnson & came
to find my way around my mother tongue
as she leaned over me, her chartreuse blouse
cut low. Mr. Stevenson
next door made no bones about his intention
of gunning down us neighbors if we sought
refuge in his bomb shelter, which resembled
a concrete slab poured for a house
without a cellar, & one day his wife
even begrudged me a token green apple
after I'd asked for it
nicely instead of picking their tree clean
one night. In the event
of an emergency,
my father said we'd simply duck
into the well room in the basement: three
people stuffed into a space twice
the size of a phone booth, with only kind
of a skylight for a window—a block
of Coke-bottle-green glass
planted in the cement outside
the back door overhead. A neighbor boy
stepped on a similar
well window on a summer day
when his feet were wet, & it blew
like a land mine
in my war comics, having magnified
the sun's heat many times. Later
the Shepherd girl
walked through a plate-glass window in a trance
while leaving church one Sunday.
At twelve I steeped myself
in the invisible & read

up on the atom Madame Curie caught
exposing itself right under
her nose, half-shot
in a negative—proof positive
of all living matter's wish to return
to a prior, glorious state of being
inert. I escaped in airplanes
I designed & drew; plus, I searched
the stars for the flying saucers
my father's loony uncle smuggled me
a paperback about—my first.
At thirteen the black book opened
at the end of each week
gave me the word the world
was doing a slow burn,
the earth reduced to ashes
in my eyes. Soon after
the Pacific island Bikini Atoll
got blown to high heaven,
the new sex bomb Bardot
& her bikini exploded
in *Life,* an Aphrodite born
of the fallout from dismembering Father
Time. What
with a scorched-earth
policy toward the future
in force, today became an end
in itself, no longer yesterday's baby
destined to grow up overnight & bring
another day into the world tomorrow.
Since nothing now would come
of it, the past remained
dead & buried, & the present
suddenly stood naked
& alone, stripped bare like the poor soul

condemned to beg asylum in the body.
I had turned fourteen, with the globe
shrinking & its population on the road
to exploding. They sent me up the river,
above Sleepy Eye & beyond
Blue Earth, to visit the first nuclear
reactor in the state. I went along
with the men in white coats who oversaw
the peaceful operation done with spotless
stainless steel, as in a modern dairy
built to mass-produce milk laced
with strontium 90. At night
I dived into the atom, but the deeper
into it I plunged, the more bits & pieces
surfaced, so I never got to the bottom
of the vortex. The particles
it gave rise to seemed to exist
(when you came down to it) in name only,
which proved enough
for me. I closed that book
the next year when I memorized a speech
against the Bomb. The teacher sitting
in judgment of me listened with a face
of stone & didn't think
I deserved to be mentioned honorably
even. Some kids
drove me home in their convertible, laughing
all the way, while I kept silent.
It wasn't long before I fell for Gertrude
Stein's name in *Time*. One day,
after I'd worked room service at the Curtis
for quarters after school, I lost
myself in the dark woods
of the still-unrazed library & brought
her words to light. The less

I understood, the happier I was.
In her hands, any given word could mean
many things, depending
on your angle, & when you saw all sides
at once, the meanings canceled one
another out. Each word became a thing
in itself, palpable as the alphabet
in soup & so
unlike the atoms that evaporated
in Wilson's cuckoo Cloud Chamber.
As far as I could tell, the world & the Word
just meant one thing: I was fated to get burned.
But if words were things, they would give me shelter,
& I could build myself a world with them
—if only a space in which to rehearse
the end of everything chance had programmed
into the beginning—as I homed in
on zero hour, when the bomb time was stopped
ticking & the great chain
reaction of days left
the earth a stone.

from THE DOUBLE HOUSE OF LIFE *(1989)*

PIRATED VERSION

Lost as usual in the shallow depths
of the pond-green aquarium
where wide-eyed guppies nose around a little
man in a diving suit beside
a minute treasure chest, the light from above

seemingly frozen & the only sound
water bubbling through the filter, I stand
to add a gold star to my name again
today by being a good boy & not
crying out for a shot of Novocain.

My mother has walked me here through the snow
—up the street, down the hill, & past
Lake Nokomis—to let Dr. Elasky
fill more of the twenty-seven
cavities he's found in my baby teeth

before I'm even five. Inside,
above the chair, he's hung some model airplanes
(a yellow Piper Cub my favorite)
from the ceiling to keep my mind
off the business at hand, but pain

always blocks them out & leaves me conscious
of nothing save his pencil-line black mustache,
plus my mother trying to quiet me
with the words, "Oh, Randy, you know
it doesn't hurt

that much." I don't know anything
yet, at least not the way knowing
just means sitting still for something
everyone says
is for the best but I feel in my bones

to be the opposite. Like a frogman
undermining a ship, I stay in the dark
below the surface & the distant static
of voices with their foreign words, seeing
by my own lights, knowing what I know.

CALLING

Researchers can duplicate any climate
but I will keep from them my little world,
the hothouse I grew up inside. The glass
my own breath steamed up made faces
back at me, minute clouds I breathed
into existence & endowed
with eyes & a mouth, as if humanizing
a snowman's blank expression. At six,
when I emerged from my fog long enough
to see something—the alphabet—was flying
in Miss Parks's class, everybody else
had got a handle on it & had learned
to exercise their liberal will to power
over words, but I was trying to come
to terms with the black marks lined up
against me in the book & then X-rayed
on the board, where black was white & vice versa.
As if following a musical score,
I had to rhyme the sounds that came
out of me & the letters with their code
of silence others took to mean they were
there to be used as tools—say by a priest
working old Mr. Stevens for his soul.
Eventually I translated my voice
to the page, just as even now my tongue
secretly shapes each word I read or write.
Since words well up inside me, I don't know
how to calculate their effect
or twist them to my ends to get whatever
leverage I desire, it may be,
at X's expense, the way certain people
will do certain things & afterwards plead
it wasn't really them—they'd merely wanted
to go from A to B by any means
at their disposal. For the life of me

I can't outline my moves
in advance any more
than I can think before opening my mouth,
so that I might not always tell the truth
but speak, for better or worse, from the heart,
as if still conversing
with my imaginary friend I dialed
on my play phone before I started school.
He or she, whose name still
escapes me, was the same as me, only
different. I could surprise myself with what
I found to say, yet be assured somebody
listened at the other end of the line.

VOWELS

Flushed out from under the mahogany
dining table where I played with my cars
among its spider legs & heard my mother
save me from the thunder
one evening with the story they were bowling
in the sky, I was first assigned a bus
with a number too big for my small mind
& then taken away from home a distance
I could cover but never would have walked
only to find myself

in school. Once at my desk, I stared at where
the inkwell dating from my parents' day
had been, a black-stained knothole no larger
than the pitch-dark *o*'s my father showed me
keyhole saws cut in pole houses designed
for sudden Y-tailed soaring purple martins.
I was so terrified
of raising my hand & asking permission
to leave my seat I wet my pants
instead, but gradually I put

two & two together: certain
letters of the alphabet were different
because they breathed life into it, like holes
I punched in the blue-&-white lid I kept
on every many-footed caterpillar
I locked up behind glass to watch grow wings,
& let me breathe out words as I sat buried
in my reader, pronouncing Dick & Jane
alive who saw Spot run &, walled in
by windows, flying with him through the pages.

RICHFIELD

The smoldering odor
of dead leaves raked against my stone foundation
tells me it's 1950 & I'm fishing
cool salamanders out

of a window well. Charcoal-black
with splotches of flesh-pink,
they look like they've survived the third-degree
burns featured in my father's *Life*

at War. That summer my uncle dropped down
on all fours in the yard, the grown-from-seed
lawn glossy as Easter
grass, & trapped a rabbit

under his hat, I wanted to keep it
out back in a cage I awoke
the next sun-shot morning to find
smeared with guts: a cat. The scene of the crime

marked the spot where a robin froze
so a kid given a Red Ryder gun
for his birthday could squeeze a gold BB
into its thumb-size head. When I confessed,

the word got chanted through the bulldozed farm
country by the Turnbull boys, whose father
I watched a court of law railroad for shooting
the dog harassing his pet fox. His eldest,

a tattooed green Marine, coasted me up
& down the block on his Harley-Davidson
one warm evening after supper, before
going to Korea. Then came the night

I didn't think I'd live
to see the day—tomorrow—I'd turn seven:
my candle-lit family of three
hugged the southwest corner

of the basement & waited for the white
lightning to nail the oak outside our door
before the wind funneled our house
into the sky. Later I saw

refrigerators lying on their sides
in the mud, too big & fat to get back
on their feet without help, & snapped
power lines crisscrossed the newly paved streets

like black snakes sunning themselves in the mild
aftermath. I went on living
in the breathing spaces
between the lines the growing suburb drew

around me, & today I turn
over this ground to find
the straight & narrow shade-dark rows
seeded with light.

WHITE BREAD

One morning I woke to apricot light
out my bedroom window in the still-vacant
lot not yet forested
with orange two-by-fours—another house
rising between us & the corner place,
where I first tasted tangerines the people
there had got from California
& dipped (if memory serves) in sugar section
by golden section. My white pj's
were neatly decorated with cowboys
riding tiny bucking broncos,
& I'd hallucinated the motif
on my papered four walls, delirious once
with measles. I remember my grandfather
eased me back asleep, as he had soothed
my mother as a girl with scarlet fever.
When I felt better, she would read to me
about the Little Green Car, & I'd listen
to the Lone Ranger on the radio
at night. In the kitchen
I found my mother working at the table
she'd painted red
herself, her square breadboard floured white.
Outside on the line, my father's white shirts
she always called the size of tents while standing
at her ironing board snapped in the breeze
like flags, & the starchy smell in the air
went to my head like pop fizz up my nose.
Filled out with wind, they blew up big as clouds
& sprinkled me with rain that gave me shivers
as they dried in the sun. The light was still
everything I could have wanted, but then
I couldn't trust the sun
to be there for me every day.
Just to get out of bed, I needed something

to anticipate before the sun set
on me, as if each day were my birthday
& I could look forward to an ivory
plastic guitar with ebony trim small
as a ukulele, two-tone
(black-&-white) cowboy boots, plus a silver-
studded black leather holster set with twin
pearly handled six-guns blond Hopalong
Cassidy made popular Saturday
mornings he fought the snow
on our first TV. Day in & day out
I came up with whatever lit a fire
under me each morning, & I harbored
what the light promised
like a secret. Setting my heart
on this or that meant I was never bored
at least, because I knew
the little thing I envisioned the day
held out was waiting. When I stopped being
satisfied with such small crumbs as my life
doled out to me
to savor, I began to put my faith
in divining the magic words
that would align the world
& my desire to be at one
with it, however briefly & in theory
only. My wish to speak
without speaking became a daily lump
in my throat, an ever-present
feeling of words about to come
to me so that I'd meet the light
on equal terms by rendering the same
in my image, the way the minuscule
shadows memory traces day by day
tell the other side of the sun's story.

GOLDEN VALLEY

My first night there I couldn't sleep
from all the goldenrod I'd sniffed,
playing war until it got dark

in the still-wild valley below our house,
where the Soo Line ran tanks to South Korea
those days my father stood to be called back

to active duty. My mother meanwhile
needled him about using every last
four-letter word in the book when he talked

to the home office. Swearing not to let
business become my life, I vowed to make
life my business, if on paper only.

Caterpillars had leveled Noble Grove
for our development, but across the tracks
the woods—beeches, maples, oaks—remained standing.

Later, when they were stripped of green & gold
& snow fell as if for good, the charred trees
our picture window displayed like a page

of upright characters showed me
how to absorb the losses mounting daily,
the red ink in our blood, & come

out burnt yet in the black
someday, letter-perfect
when everything was said & done.

DOUBLE LIFE

I used to live
for Sunday, when the funny papers came
in color. All week
the world was black & white, from the landscape
our picture window framed—snow (it was always
winter) spiked with wrought-iron
trees—to the choice of drinks
at the table: coffee
(black) for the grown-ups & icy milk
for us kids. Sundays brought me Dick
Tracy's crazy yellow hat, not to mention
his freckled sidekick Sam's
purple bowtie & green sports
jacket. No one I knew went around dressed
like them, but I never thought twice
about it. The whole idea
was they were free
to play with shades
of meaning, like a child
fiddling with the dials
of a color TV when nobody
is watching. I was eight,
& I had learned to read
after it hit me halfway through first grade
my world had gone to pieces (twenty-six,
to be exact). One day
I raised my hand to find them all lined up—
the "big" letters above the "small"—& marching
around the schoolroom, chalked
on a narrow frieze-like band of blackboard
nailed to the walls. Still, I asked my father
to read me the funnies those movie-bright
mornings before we joined a church, & after
we'd wrestle in the living room. Each time
our roughhousing ended with him

pinning me to the floor,
where I'd lie paralyzed
as if in an iron lung & stop breathing
under his weight. The next day he would go
& disappear for one more week—
"on the road," we called it. While he was gone,
my mother & I walked
everywhere, & she took my mind
off the perpetual sub-zero weather
by pointing out that I could see
my breath, which clued me in
to the spiritual dimension
of things & showed me to keep my eyes open
for the invisible. If, as she kept
saying, life was what I made it,
I'd have to breathe
life into things, colored as they would be
by my view of them. Soon I began hunching
over a globe & studying its colors,
in my own world at last. I never knew
our words paint the earth according
to our lights, until the world has its own
story to tell, pieced together
from all of ours, like that stained-glass
chapel in Paris where the sun
illuminates the various Bible stories
going around the room. I picture myself
smoking like a chimney
in the cold, walking through the snow
like a character in a comic strip
still on the drawing board, the cloud
of hot air ballooning from my mouth empty
yet expressive of my secret desire
to breathe a word.

KINGDOM COME

I held my breath
waiting for spring: the rising undercurrent
of melted snow taking my street
by storm, & the sun no longer
someone's idea of a joke but something
capable of bringing down the palace
of ice the cold had raised by working night
& day for what had seemed
an eternity. Meanwhile, people said
I had my whole life ahead of me,
& I believed them. Early
mornings my mother whispered in my ear
to wake up, I stumbled through the motions
of preparing myself
for school & heard her busy in the kitchen.
As if still dreaming, I'd sit
down then as now
to my half of a pink grapefruit
dusted with sugar, which gave it the kind
of rosy glow the snow took on
once the mahogany dark outside
had turned to smoke & before the sallow
light of day broke
the gloom like the headlights
of the black-numbered pumpkin school bus
lumbering down the road to stop for me,
its brakes squeaking the way, at every step,
the frozen ground would creak
like the hall floor at home
under the ugly, buckled-up
black galoshes I couldn't wait
to deposit in the cloakroom,
my last name neatly printed in blue ink
on a tiny white adhesive strip
inside each one. I lived

for the future so long the present got
to be a dream, a dress
rehearsal for a play not meant to be
performed, & only tomorrow
was real. In time I wrote
off today & imagined myself living
in a world to come. Just as I always kept
my Johnny Pesky fielder's glove
well lubricated with neat's-foot
oil all winter, I nursed my desire for spring
& learned to lay up treasure, in my words,
against a day I had no hope of seeing.

DIVINING ROD

Winters I practiced swinging my Al Kaline
Louisville Slugger in the living room
mirror, trying to keep a level bat
whether the pitcher in my mind

threw down & out or up & in. When summer
after summer saw me look good
striking out every chance I got, I traded
my lumber for a Venus No. 2.

In hopes of making contact & a name
for myself after all, I grooved my strokes
across each page, delineating features
I dreamed were mine. At first I couldn't draw

from memory, which I wrote off as pure
imagination then but now follow
to the end, a blind man
trusting where my stick leads.

WITHIN LIMITS

I never learned
to follow the music, always out of step
with what was spinning at each Friday hop

the way my heart, decades
down the road, skips a beat repeatedly
& counterpoints time's goose step round the clock.

To join the dance in everybody's blood,
I had to make my own music
as when, counting syllables at my desk

those nights as many years
ago, I found my ten fingers perfect
for playing variations on the beat

that pulses through the feet of a long line
of dancers who filled in the blank
with their own signatures.

NORTH END

1. January Country

Crows rule the roost, black as the ice
glazing a no-name pond
at the point a spring continues

feeding into it. Snow
whites out even the trees, sticking
to their trunks like the paint some old wives' tale

says scares off gypsy moths. My thoughts
take a turn for the worse, & I recall
the day that did this, all those people going,

*As I live & die, the sky has a mind
to bury us!* Flakes thick as stars on the flag
settled like ashes on the smoking houses . . .

Only now something clicks
in my head, like the cold turnstile
of another season locking

behind me. *Where to from here?* Much as
the freezing air drives the carp in the pond
deeper into their element, the stillness

turns me to words. Crows punctuate the white
like periods that sentence me
to what I've said.

2. Gray Matter

Overnight, March
invades January,
& the ice starts to break

in its wake. Mist lifts off the gray river
like dreams evaporating in the light,
like the spirit of the water rising

as a ghost to hover
above it—proof
the invisible lives.

All day, in one corner
of my mind, the vision builds up
like the pearl of the sky.

3. February Anniversary

Bare forked maples blacken in winter rain
as if possessed by their shadows,
like mourners all gathered around a grave

in silence. Fog clouds my view
of a white lake
through the trees: it's a scene

straight out of a hazy Japanese scroll
painting of a moment of change
frozen in time to remind me

of loss. Yet the harder
I have to look, the more clearly
I see. Peering

into the distance of the other shore,
I drift off across the water
to condense myself, like ink on a page.

AN ALBUM FAMILY

1

A good-time Charlie from the start, my father
wasn't even a year when he got caught
laughing at the whole idea of being
here: the black hole
of his mouth swallows the light whitening
his baby bonnet, circa 1912.

The *o* his lips have formed
is shaded like a zero on an early
printout, dark as the light-starved snow-draped earth
sledge-hammered open to the sun
fifty-two years later at Fort Snelling
or as these letters, my own charred remains.

2

Last night I'd shaved my beard & played the baby-
faced infant in the black-&-white where I'm
cheek to cheek with my mother in her floral
print dress. My lips twisted into a smile,
her faraway look says she can't conceive
what's happened to her. She stretched out her arms

& cried in my dream, begging me again
to bring her back to life. It seems the flowers
that climb all over her like shadows spring
from the leafy vines covering her chair
& papering her living room at home,
the same way I'm growing out of her hands.

THE AFTERLIFE

1. Last Spring

I stuck my nose into a hornet's nest
of blossoming wisteria, & the scent
presented me with Fleer's
sugar-coated baseball-card gum

my mother bought me in my quest
for my heroes at eleven
whenever she would stop
at Noble Drug for L & M's

some thirty years ago. Late in the day
I called her up
in Florida & learned she'd had more trouble
breathing. When I lied the sun-blackened lilacs

here were still holding on, she turned
the clock back sixty years
& smelled the long-gone white
lilacs at home one last time in my words.

2. Earthbound

My father used an alias
while still in high school to play semi-pro
baseball on Sunday so that his God-fearing
parents, who didn't smoke

or drink or even read the funny papers
on the Sabbath, wouldn't see his name Monday
morning in the box score & know he'd broken
one more commandment carved in stone.

In the future—when he mowed the grass, say,
in lieu of church—he always swore,
The better the day, the better the deed,
even to the minister's face.

His sole hope of any life after death
coming to him rested on his stories
I'd taken to heart, hallowing his name
by worshiping the sun in so many words.

STARFISH

1
They caught my eye today, the shoals
of fire-thorn berries coral-orange
in clear September light, & I remembered

coast-hugging robins will depend on them
to make it back to spring. Sunset flaring
salmon-pink now, my enlarged heart

jumps like a red mullet
when I think of the fish
swimming in your belly as of this morning.

2
A prairie child hearing the sea,
I press my ear to your belly
as to a bleached conch shell. Sounding

your depths, I am my father listening
for the life-&-death difference
between whales & Japanese submarines

forty-two years ago
on his destroyer in the South Pacific,
months before I was born. Tonight, sonar

gives shape to what waits to torpedo you:
a skull-white globe trails clouds of swirling snow
in the dark, ghostly as a colorless

TV's fluttery picture of the earth
shot from space, & I pinpoint the future
on the screen where

an infinitesimal heart
pulses like the center of a starfish,
like the eye of a hurricane on radar.

3
Out here, under the stars—
I mean, there in the night
where it's all being out

together this winter a microdot
at a time, minnow-quick & inching forward
by leaps & bounds. Ten digits to my name,

I was once my warring father's only proof
of divinity. Then my mother called
into the distance, "When it happens

to me," & I pretended not
to hear, as if still just a child
whose mother couldn't die. Up above, nothing

ever goes wrong, while down below we are
wrong from the word *go*: they're nothing but
chancy, our combinations in the dark.

4
You wonder what the future will look like.
As my good aunt said at my mother's funeral,
"What else is there

but resemblance?" It unearths such relations
(family or otherwise) as teach us
the world is not carved in granite

but something we envision in the raw
material at hand & build up
invisibly inside by constantly

discovering our ever-changing place
in it, which hinges on the granddaddy
of four-letter words: *like.*

5
This evening you fit the curve of my hand
perfectly, & trying
to put my finger on what slips

out from under my thumb
like a tropical fish at large inside
a dark aquarium, I'm small

again & feel the world
spin in my palm
back there in my grandfather's dim   ·

extra room, playing roulette with his globe
to see its many colors break
down into countries

that stop & linger at my finger tips
an instant at a time, as if
within easy reach, like plum-shaded Turkey.

Now, when I picture your infinitely finite
skin diver probing every inch
of space as if to touch bottom

in your landlocked sea, the child I was falls
asleep once more imagining
the borders of the universe.

6
A high-flying jet cutting the blue down
to size stitches east & west together
like a spider, its silk-white thread unraveling

as it goes. From his post in a bloomed cherry,
a hawk-eyed robin scrambles to fight off
dive-bombing jays intent on raiding

his nest of loose ends in a neighboring
long-needled pine, where his black-headed mate
broods unflinching. Let that be you.

7
"Like waiting for the Bomb
to drop," the doctor jokes, meaning the baby
expected any day hangs over you

like a nameless descendant of Type-A
"Little Boy" born out of the blue
forty-odd years before.

8
It begins with a distant cry
like a bird's I can't believe I have heard
in the dark before dawn early in spring,

& soon the blood-shot purple face
of something, eyes
puckered shut, surfaces from its lagoon.

Flushed out of hiding, your chameleon
changes in the light: dawn-rosy fingers
turn baby shrimp, pearl toes lilies

of the valley. Day One he plays
close to the vest, clinging
to my chest like a ladybug. His head

is fuzzy like an apricot & round
as a fat McIntosh.
His eyes are blueberries.

He cries like water seething to a boil,
& he hiccups like so many
Champagne corks popping New Year's Eve.

Mouth like the sweet calyx of a day lily,
little fists like peony buds, nipples
shadowy as the moon

in daylight, heart beating
like a hummingbird's wings, he dives
into your breast.

9
He eats like a bird, a downy-
headed duckling
blindly open-mouthed. He himself

is warm & buttery, like a hot loaf
of my grandmother's bread. Grandfathers nothing
but bones anymore breathe again

in his chest, lips, & cheeks, his breath pure
wintergreen. Seashells for ears, he wrinkles
up his face like a quince, for he grows

quizzical before all things. His wizened
far-off gaze reflects the distance
he has come in nine months. His eyes

look the smoky midnight-blue of the sky
at dusk today, Venus cradled
by May's crescent moon glowing with the milky

aura of its future. I wish him luck
as good as mine that he fell like a star
into my arms.

REFUGE

A stand of paper birches years & years
of lovers have tattooed with their black hearts
& initials shades the starved baby tapping
his mother's breast like a downy woodpecker.

In the marsh behind him, red-winged blackbirds
go down in flames to feed
cattail-sheltered nestlings while bullfrogs
tune their bass instruments, as if rehearsing

for the night ahead. Here, where generations
have come to leave their mark
in passing, the plus signs
still add up to something like desire:

all the letters of the alphabet
in love with one another to this day.

from GRAPHIC SCENES *(1994)*

THE ACOLYTE

At thirteen, just before the sunrise service
ended with the customary prayer
for the health of President Eisenhower,
I read verses from St. Paul's Ephesus

chapter, suddenly in love with the letters
I found clustered on bread-white Bible leaves
like black Concord grapes, & I rolled them around
on my tongue, without thinking what they meant

beyond their shape & sound. It was the body
of words that I desired, & I partook
of them as if they were the flesh & blood
of the spirit that gave me life, because

they translated—when, in due time, they came
from me—the world into my terms & made
a place in it for me at last, a likely
story I imagined for myself.

COLOR VALUES

The trees go to blazes—cranberry swamp
maples, pumpkin birches, honey
sycamores. Once the sun
peaked in June, it was all downhill
into the fire for them, & in the spirit

of fall I burn to see myself at ten
shoulder again my uncle's double-barreled
twelve-gauge my father had me point
at the lowest branch of a gilded oak
off the Cass Lake road, my black Labrador

frozen in her tracks & my mother's voice
a whisper coaching me
not to pull but squeeze the trigger: one blast
reduced a family of partridges
to dust. Looking at what I'd done

with birdshot, I had seen enough to last
a lifetime, doomed as I believed I was
when I found their minute pin
feathers delicately tinged
cinnamon, as if someone loved them also.

PERSONAL HISTORY

A pre-med grad the Crash plunged into selling
the Delta seed before getting commissioned
& shipped out to the war, my father wound
up a "rag" man—his grandfather who joined
the Union Army had set sail from Hamburg

a tailor—& thus steered me toward German
classes for their value to the doctor
I, at least, would be, but when blue-eyed Miss
Snabbi (her given name, Grace, off-limits)
read us eternal sophomores Wolfgang Borchert

& Gottfried Benn, who in their words
sifted through the ashes
of a future gone up in smoke,
the spirit of the letters she translated
dovetailed with my sense I would burn

tomorrow, my name written down
with the black mark of having life too good
against it in the Book, & I began
to dream not of escaping fate
but of rewriting it to make it mine.

Just as my German family name sounded
English to me—I can still hear my father
telling somebody on the phone, "It's *Blazing*
but with an *s*"—I would find my own way
into the flames.

CHAMBERS OF THE HEART

Since I know by heart the floor plan
of every house I grew up in,
I follow in my own footsteps

& enter the living room now of house
number two, where I re-shot with cap guns
our first TV's Saturday-morning version

of Custer's last stand to my satisfaction,
& my father zoomed in on the small screen
to size up big-talking Joe McCarthy.

When, in the dining L, my mother lunched
with girlfriends winter afternoons, I played
alone under the table, in the five-

o'clock shadow of all those legs. The hall
between the bedrooms framed my silhouette
snipped out at Dayton's in a flash, eyelashes

intact. Just as I made the rounds of past
houses, memorizing their ins & outs
like someone going blind, I move, as though

by plan, from room to room on this blueprint,
still a black figure on a light background,
& measure off my future home.

THREE HOUSES

And look! My last, or
next-to-last, of three loved houses went.
Elizabeth Bishop

1. Benefit Street

Up on the "almost pastoral" East Side
of town, where door after door bears the sign
of the Guardian Angel ("24-Hour

Surveillance & Security"), I duck
between the bas-relief Ionic columns
straddling the threshold of the Federal house

I've called mine ten years this April. Palm Sunday
come & gone yesterday, what as a child
I thought was "Monday" Thursday, then Good Friday
—days holy only as I remember them—

beat time at its own game. My future mortgaged,
I made my home in history inside
these four walls on a hill & said I could
imagine dying here, reborn at forty.

2. Kyle Avenue

Again last night I sank up to my knees
into my native ground in Minnesota,
& it appeared my mother had bequeathed
to me our east-facing third house, complete

with the warm & fuzzy African violets
she raised in pots on a wrought-iron cart
inside the picture window, the room white
as my whole dream. After my father died

when I was twenty, vultures cleaned her out,
& she got hate mail like a ransom note
for selling to a black-&-white couple.

Moving, she scattered me to the four winds,
giving away ten years of baseball cards
& my Erector Set & Beat the Clock.

3. Twenty-Second

Growing up, I celebrated the only
Easter warm enough to hunt eggs outdoors,
looting the backyard of my mother's house
where Nana hid for me a plastic bunny.
I squeezed its tail, breathing life into it,
& goosed it into jumping, pink like my pet
white rabbits' eyes I met at home each morning
behind the chicken wire of their blue hutch.

But soon a farmer came to take them all
off my father's hands, & I heard Grandpa
had gone like his black-spotted springer, Patsy,
the dark Easter of Joe DiMaggio's bat
& a ball autographed by Marty Marion.
Then I was ten, the house a memory.

HARDBALL

After barrel-chested Earl Torgeson
(my father's favorite) & workmanlike
polite Bill Tuttle (my mother's) had vanished
into the bus in the shadows outside
Comiskey Park, I stood
asking my idol, Al
Kaline, how to connect with the curve balls
I had already seen coming at twelve,
& he answered
shyly, a twenty-one-year-old crew-cut
blond "phenom" speaking from experience,
You have to find

your own way. It happened my way
would mean stealing a page from the curves' book
& winding down—as on a spiral stair—
into the ground along the lines
of the biggest curve imaginable,
which ends up in the dirt. No star, I knew
I'd never rise above the earth,
but sometimes I'd feel light-headed descending
on the spin my English put on each step
I took. In a word, I would make a virtue
of necessity, which, like rules,
freed me to play the game I'd choose.

AT LENGTH

Grounded, I watched late-breaking spring take off
without me in the yard. Nightly in March
a cardinal staking out his territory
under my bedroom woke me to the darkness
before dawn with his incessant wolf whistles.

On the eve of Easter a wave of black-masked
cedar waxwings, tail feathers tipped the gold
of each incipient Norway-maple leaf,
harrowed the earth, devouring as they went
fallen crab apples shriveled up like cherries.

Then, on May Day, the second oriole
of my life flashed across the lawn & dived
into the nettled, coral-flowering quince.
I took his fence-sitting mate for a vireo,
camouflaged as she was in drab olive.

Somewhere along the line, an orange-breasted
cock-of-the-walk a robin's size left me
speechless, & I looked him up—a towhee—
the way as a kid back in Minnesota
I passed long winters that kept spring on hold

leafing through a field guide. I came to know
birds I couldn't hope to see but started
repeating the names of—*indigo bunting,*
scarlet tanager—as a kind of song
I chanted silently, testing my wings.

COUNTRY SONG

Every shade of gray, your scales remind me
—though the scale is wrong—of a hoot owl's feathers,
& once, your black-lace wings
extended on a salt-&-pepper couch
where you snoozed camouflaged & I joined millions
cheering another summer's games in Rome
(the screened words courtesy of Olivetti),
I saw a dragonfly in you. Today,

when I awoke in a sweat at first light,
you started harping on what stings you deepest
morning to night. I had driven roads black
with ice, through fields blanked out by snow,
to my mother's failed heart again & cried
when my father was reduced to smoked meat . . .

You have your life mapped out for you, designed
so thoughtfully (down to your tail's point white
like the bird-lime ellipses finch & sparrow
chalk on slate-smooth bark to mark their absence)
that you become invisible to all
intents & purposes—save killer wasps?—
against this particular silver olive,
whose precious shade keeps the demon sun

from going to my head at noon. No Horace
swearing off wine, I still find my buzz comes
from you who drum your song into my head,
& soon I only hear my voice
singing my one note to myself as I
likewise practice not being here, cicada.

LIFELINES

Wind scorches the dirty-blond earth
receiving the Temple
of Dionysus, whose columns shored up
by cement are marble
twenty centuries have weathered a cross
between the ashen trunks
of the still-standing olive trees
& their quicksilver leaves, as Teos returns
to dust surrounded by an endless grove

of mandarin oranges. When I dusted
myself off in the lime-green sea
opposite a beach gold in name
only, the water was so cold
it scalded me, the way I burned my tongue
licking a freezing monkey bar
gray as a pencil lead four decades back
below my mother's house deep in the City
of Lakes. Learning to hold my tongue early,

I hearkened to her stories of the figures
she'd cut as a girl skating into the dark,
scratching the surface of snow-dusted ice
lined like these moon-white
rectangles underfoot I now zigzag,
digging up shadowy traces
of cryptic letters written
in stone—the black magic
that keeps souls alive when the sky caves in.

PERMANENT INK

The sun shrinking to a vanishing point
of light gives me a jolt, like the small shock
the faulty wiring of my heart
shoots through it now
& then. Where a little child sees an *o*

for *orange,* I find a black hole
my days feed into, one by one, the way
words sentenced to stand together for life
come down to a period's needle-eye zero
nothing passes through. In the next breath

sparks fly across the sky
I gaze into as if wishing
upon my future in a shining well
of ink, & the scene goes dark as these letters
suffused, in their time, by so many shades.

HYMN TO THE SUN

I
Sleeping within earshot of the Aegean
once more, I forget where I am
a second & mistake the surf's white noise
for rain, unheard-of here

in summer. July Fourth, & the fireworks
all the apricot stars provide
leave me oohing & ahing like my mother
watching the real thing with me at North Commons

when I was eight. The child
conceived but inconceivable
in this house a year ago is two months
into his—& our—new life. Though he's present

in the flesh, he's still not to be believed:
his feet are the same color, size, & shape
as Eberhard erasers, perfect
for scuffing out any trace of his father's

footsteps. When birds applaud the sunrise, one big
coral rose unfolding, his blue eyes open
like morning glories, & he smiles, face breaking
into light like a sunflower.

II
Back at the Fisherman's Hotel in ancient
Halicarnassus for another summer
ten years ago, I woke up our first morning

& found our old boatman's
Antioch (named for his hometown) was missing
from the line-up of small craft all along

the shore. By noon we'd heard the news: asleep
or drunk, he'd fallen overboard last night
& drowned (he always joked he couldn't swim),

while his group of Americans below
slept peacefully & drifted until dawn.
That afternoon, we watched men carry him,

wrapped in a green cloth like a movers' pad
crisscrossed with rope, & take turns shouldering
his dead weight through the streets for no more

than seven steps apiece—one for each day
of the weeks that run away with our lives?—
in a kind of frantic dance that went on

until they got where they were bearing him,
& we continued, for the moment, walking
the opposite direction in the circle.

III
Outside NATO's mirrored Southeast Command
Headquarters, the flags of many
nations stand saluting
the wind off the olive-
drab sea. One of the MP's on guard duty

squeezes his Uzi & smiles to himself
at his good luck to be ogling
the legendary women of Izmir,
not waiting for the dust to rise
back in some Hittite village buried deep

in Anatolia. Meanwhile, a boy
with a rubber shoe on one foot
& a blue plastic sandal on the other
peddles the golden local variation
of sesame bagels stacked up to look

braided together on the big square tray
he balances on his head, round face freckled
as with those selfsame seeds, & a grown man
on a bike crates a honeycomb
of brown eggs through traffic

as though they were gold. On the quai
this morning, a guy hangs over the side
of a freighter, painting the *s* in *Tigris*
the very blue
the water was just twenty years

ago but is today
only in postcards of the modern city,
& he is in his own world as I am
in mine, misrepresenting everything
I put in words as if I were at home.

IV
Home after the birth, I entered our bedroom
alone & saw the handwriting
on the wall: the photographs nailed to it

were doomed. No more
shots one of us had taken of the other,
like the black-&-white you got of me staring

back at myself
in the Huntington's lily pond
—my shadow burned into a sheet of paper—

& no more inhuman
landscapes like the sun-tanned blue vista
you froze in Cappadocia

of a lone tree in a potato field
backed by a not-so-grand
canyon & Mount Argaeus, still snow-crowned

in August. We'd stopped our beige Hertz Renault
& stolen the season's last apricot
dangling from a branch no one, to our knowledge,

guarded, when a young man on a red bike
rode out of nowhere, eager
to talk. People were strong

around there, he said, but life was so hard
on his plateau that all of them wore out
by thirty-five, his voice as gravelly

as the mountain stream we'd heard when we lay
down beside it
earlier in the day, sick as tourists . . .

Thinking out loud, I told myself
we'd soon stick pictures of the newcomer
around the room & populate each future

view with him. For now, he lies & studies
an olive tree at sea in the wind, eyes
dancing, arms & legs churning away,

ecstatic. He sees leaf upon leaf flutter
like his small fingers in response, my own
ten fingers composing this candid picture.

V
Diamond-blue Venus trapped
between the prongs

of tonight's white-gold crescent moon
can't hold a candle to the flash points

of the baby's eyes now as he examines
his hand like a jeweler sizing up

a precious stone, or an astronomer
discovering a star.

VI
Outside the door, a lamb on death row bleated
through the night like someone with the dry heaves.
In the morning he's sacrificed to Allah:
hogtied, blindfolded, throat slit, all the little
children suffered to watch (life not being
for the squeamish). They flinch perceptibly
as the lamb jerks his last & bleeds & bleeds,
Isaac's stand-in even at this late date

in history. Turning away, I hear
a rushing sound somewhere—water fanning
out across cracked dry earth? The eyes
beat ears as witnesses, wrote Heraclitus:
red fire sweeps through brown weeds nearby,
the one true god making its presence known.

VII
Each time the baby tugs
on his bottle, I feel his tongue

work the nipple like a sunfish
nibbling the bait at the end of my line

when I was small & trolled
Leech Lake with my father.

VIII
I dream of taking our small son to visit
your father's grave, an oversize bee box
topped with a round enameled porcelain
likeness of him not long before he died

at thirty-two. Above our heads the pines
that should be cypresses thrive on the lack
of water, old as death (not these
particular examples but their kind).

As I imagine remembering the scene,
our son is big enough to stand
in the dust & hang on my thumb the way
you clutched your father's hand thirty years before.

He slipped through your fingers into dark air
like a helium balloon you forgot
not to let go of as a little girl
leaving the fair at nightfall in his arms.

IX
Last night I dreamed I'd lost you, & my life
was over, too. After all, you showed me
how to live, teaching me to look at things

I'd never seen. My grief at losing you
was like my panic at the thought
of going blind. Sharp-eyed

as the sun, you zero in on the sparrow's
every feather where, at one point, I didn't
even see a sparrow. Not a single
particular beneath
your notice, you quicken
each minute with your minute observations.
Lost in detail? Not on your life! Without
details, I'm lost & don't know where time goes.

Yesterday I paid a routine visit
to the village fountain—a roadside spigot
I would have missed if not watching
for it—& saved the day
by opening my eyes to a mundane
vision. Surrounded by red plastic buckets
& silver pails, light-darkened faces lined
like the cracked end-of-August earth, three women
squatted on their haunches in ordinary
floral-print dresses—morning glories, orange
poppies, smoky tobacco leaves—& what
teeth they had left gleamed in the sun: gold.
Were they the Fates confirming that my life
is flashing like a dream before my eyes?

X
September means it's twenty years ago
this month I swam in salt water
here the first time in my life, hot springs veining
the marbled sea. Since then, I've dipped

into San Clemente's gold-flecked Pacific
& had the wind shocked out of me
by Maine's Atlantic at Acadia,
cold & clear as machine-made ice. The sea

isn't the enemy fresh water was
in Minnesota: there, I never thought
I'd learn to swim, dunked in chlorine while clinging
to the end of my rope

all winter &, each summer, thrown
into a lake, where sinking to the muddy
bottom was like imagining
polio. My salty

tears of fear & disappointment that showed
what others called my true colors in fact
proved I had it in me to stay afloat
when I found myself at sea in the world.

I only had to discover my points
of correspondence with it & I'd surface
in my element, buoyed by my inner
resources on the salt-white page.

XI
I was past forty when I harvested
my first olives this September, the tree
in question not a hundred yet & still
a baby. Spotting their black beauty marks

like periods that call an end
to their growing season, I went
out on a limb & reached the clustered fruits
peeping through the leaves like green eyes hidden

behind silver veils. The tree stands for peace
because it lives forever & its gifts
sustain so many morning, noon, & night.

Bent over backward now along the lines
of tonight's equinoctial gale, it gives
shape to the wind.

XII
Stars mist the blacked-out sky the last night
of September like gold dust carried off
by desert winds, one more summer's

treasure of days scattered
out of reach & reduced
to grains of sand the bully time is kicks

in my face. My head spins
with constellations drawn about as finely
as patterns in a Turkish rug that borders
on embroidery & grounds my eyes in what

lies under my nose. I have tried to weave
such a spell myself by tracing each thread
that ties me to the farthest star, a point
of light that comes to a point in my hands.

FADED KODACHROME

Every last leaf has fallen from the trees
around the darkened pond, a grit-scarred lens
that focuses the spotty washed-out blue
above. Dropping from the sky, a mallard
hits the skids as he applies the brakes,
stopping short on the water like a Corsair
landing, flaps down, on a carrier
in my father's day. My son falls for leaves
glinting like Lincoln pennies on the ground.
In the habit of finding signs
of resurrection everywhere
I turn, I mistake an airborne orange
beech leaf for a long-lived monarch
before I catch myself & think: *Too late.*

The woods have faded like a Kodachrome,
the way the farther I go back in album
time, the less colorful the characters
under the sun, till shades of gray
sink the family tree in mist & shadows.
Each step I take chasing my son
into the future puts that much more distance
between us in the book. Grabbing a minute,
we rest on what I teach him is a *stump,*
& the wind howling all around us barks
up any tree, right or wrong. Once, the light
was everything; now it's the wind,
hustling me off toward the day
when I will take my stand in black & white.

BURIAL GROUNDS

1. Historical Cemetery

My mother always mourned the childlessness
of her lone brother for the simple fact
their family name would die with him, as if
she came from some unbroken royal line.
The baby boy who keeps my name alive
unbeknownst to her plays among the graves
of two-hundred-year-old strangers who've put
their hearts & souls into a copper beech
that shelters them from God's own sky at last,
but in the meantime here below
the elements have cost them all their names.

Walking the rows of upright white
tablets wind & rain have erased
& restored to their original state
of blank slates, my gleeful son pats them each
on the head, as if he were a grown-up
& they small children inching up on him.
From where I stand, the page-shaped slabs
I momentarily darken with my shadow
as though with my name appear
thin as this paper I must trust
to outlast flesh & blood, let alone stone.

2. Gray Area

My infant son haunts the cemetery
& plays peek-a-boo with stones white
as the blank faces of so many swimmers
trying to keep their heads above water.

Watching him disappear
behind a certain marker, I make out
his given name writ large, a boy his age
who, I read, "unfortunately drown'd

in infancy" & whose
poor father, middle-aged like me two short
centuries ago, followed him I see
to an early grave the next year. The shallow

letters cut in rock look the same
tattletale-gray as my own name the sun
once filled with shadows as fast as the child
I was could trace it in the snow.

3. Breaking the Ice

Visiting the dead, my son walks on water—
i.e., snow crusted with knife-edged ice
of the kind that almost took off the top
of my head when I sailed
into it on my Flexible
Flyer &, picking myself up
off the floor of the valley, came home blinded
by tears & blood. Toward sundown

the growing shadows of the tapered stones
point accusing fingers at me
standing tall there as my boy, small enough
to play hide-&-seek among them,
skates across the glaring surface
I break with every step of my cold feet.

SETTING OUT

for John-John

You won't remember how we walked tonight
after you cried, your *Little Golden Book*
of Planets under your arm, "Let's go out
on the earth & see what
is there!" Under the moon you'd found egg-shaped

with only a handful of words
last year, owls announced their unseen presence
—a hiss alternating with a deep sigh,
like your heavy breathing
when you sleep off another long hard day—

& crickets lying low
rolled their *r*'s around us in the grass,
while the stars I saw highlight the Big Dipper
struck you as flashes in my DAR
grandmother's black fry pan where I cook up

your Sunday flapjacks. When in the end
you summarized the world
so far—"Then on the earth
are owls & crickets, & in the sky, stars?"—
I listened to how still things were

above the undercurrent of the sea
coming & going like my blood I'd heard
slosh back & forth on an echocardiograph
before your time, my irregular heart
a weathered craft straining at its frayed line.

WHOLE LIFE

When my son watered down strays with his long-shot
squirt gun from the patio after dinner,

I peered into the dark until I saw
my father in his Skivvies shirt & boxers

aim my air rifle at the tom that slaughtered
the baby robins in our weeping willow

his last summer. The nights his aching heart
kept him from sleep, I awoke, too, & listened

as the boy he'd been watched a Minnesota
River suck hole swallow his friend, & witnessed

Doc Duclos raised from his own shit each April,
the squaw he'd shacked up with gone at the thaw.

Just as the stories that my father told
let him round out his life, his origins

as close to him as he'd come to his end,
the tales I spin this way bring me full circle.

SECOND LANGUAGE

. . . love begins at the point when a woman
enters her first word in our poetic memory.
Milan Kundera

The smallest green chameleon
gone with a flick
of its tongue returns me

to our beginnings
& brings back the first time
twenty-five years ago you ran

across the English word for it
& asked me what it meant.
When I explained it stood

for change, you wondered
what would become of us,
& I heard myself say

for my part I would go
on loving you, language
I'd never used in all my days.

THE SUMMER HOUSE

(Dalyan Village, Turkey, 1990)

1. Unscheduled Flight

At dawn I go down to Homer's Aegean
& find barn swallows cutting figure eights
above a field of yellow gorse, purple
burdock, oxeye daisies, various shades
of starry eyebright, yarrow, & wild carrot.
Scything the air, they live on what no mortal
eye can see, & take me back twenty years
to the Piazza Michelangelo
in Florence at dusk, when I saw these birds
thriving on the invisible as spirits
rising & falling above Dante's Arno,
tails forked like the gold nibs of Grandpa's
fountain pens I dipped into at eight
& filled with Sheaffer's ink as blue as swallows.

2. Descent

When I see how fast the sun disappears
behind the mountains of Chios, gone all
at once like an orange rolled off the edge
of a table, I begin to grasp the speed
I'm flying through my days, with faith in nothing
but the light. That reminds me of the story
of Johnny, Arthur, Tony—RAF
fly-boys who stopped on their last leave & tossed me
into the air at my Welsh grandfather's
before they flew back home, only to vanish
in fog returning from a German raid
or meet with friendly fire crossing the Channel,
nobody there to catch them when they fell.
They swim before my eyes, names black as floaters.

3. *Sunday Pagan*

This is the kind of day I'll die recalling.
Flush with the atmosphere at last, the air
the same temperature as my body now,
I warm to a sea neither blue nor green,
not sky or earth but something in between,
the holy water that baptizes me
in the one life of the four elements.
On the same wavelength as the sun, I burn
as if I had all the time in the world,
summer convincing me I'm of a piece
with things in spirit for a day or season.
Intensified, the light transfixes me,
as when I feel a spell is coming on
& fall into a trance, a little song.

4. *Fishing Village Farewell*

The sea the color of petroleum,
waving white flags of surrender, proclaims
this summer's fall. Across the gulf, the island
lost in the mist of distance since the solstice
closes in. September, & time to clear
out, a chill in the blood & war once more
in the air. I'll never finish horse-starved
Xenophon's journey home through Kurdistan,
I tell myself, & capture my son flanked
by two friends in a parting shot as they
glare back into the last of the sun, light
catching them like the sultana-gold net
some fisherman enmeshed in his lines mends
all afternoon beside the still backwaters.

VISIONARY COMPANY

Last night when our son said, "The two of you
are beautiful," I knew he wasn't falling
for how the shadows at our candle-lit

dinner for three erased the lines the years
have raked across our faces, but perhaps
buttering us up & learning to trade

words for love. Putting myself in his place,
I sat back at the right hand of my father,
who manfully watched me play his opposite

versus his understudy, as when, my hair
silvered for *King Lear*'s Kent like his, it happened
I kissed him good-bye on the mouth for good,

& across the blond table from my mother,
whose blue shadow-box hung over my head
& in whose teal-flecked eyes I could do no wrong,

wrong as I was in so much that I did
or failed to do, like telling her the fall
she died I'd be a father in the spring.

I saw my parents vanish in the time
it took our candle to burn down to nothing
—both, to my mind, beautiful in that light.

GRAPHIC SCENES

1. Mother Tongue

When I was growing up, my mother lip-
synched everything I said, as if I played
Charlie McCarthy to her Edgar Bergen
on an *Ed Sullivan Show* tape reversed.
Reading her lips, which trembled as they did
bristling with pins whenever she cut out
a midnight-blue pattern, I watched my words
come back to haunt me like an echo made

visible. Like those lettered souls dumbstruck
Augustine saw mouth Scripture silently,
she'd repeat my syllables to herself
as gospel. Shadowing my speech, she taught me
to listen while I spoke, so that one day
I'd talk like this, without moving my lips.

2. Man of Letters

Blank scrolls of waves unfolding at his feet,
my five-year-old scratches his name with sandstone
on tablets he no sooner fishes out
of the water than the sea wipes them clean,
much as the dizzy smoke-blowing pilot
overhead chalks backward letters on the sky
high-flying wind erases at the speed
breath-clouds evaporate from a mirror:

who doesn't burn to leave his mark? As good
as fifty, my days spent translating myself
into indelible ink.& vice versa,
I can't tell the strokes of my razor-point
from blood. My signature resembles nothing
more than my heartbeat on an EKG.

3. Last Words

My father never thought that he would die
of natural causes but always believed
he'd meet his end on the road, seeing how
he drove a hundred thousand miles a year.
Yet he beat the odds on an accident
only to get blind-sided by his heart,
sitting in his forest-green La-Z-Boy
while watching *Gunsmoke* in his oak-paneled den.

My mother reported on his deathbed
he tried, cool to the last, to help the doctors
find his pulse. That's when Brother Patrick prayed,
speeding me there in his blue Malibu,
but I recited lines I knew by heart,
drumming up a beat to bring back my father.

4. Cardiogram

Chances are good my number will be up
before my kindergarten son ever
graduates from high school, my doctor hints,
given my scores on my latest blood test.
In the past, she let me have the Bible's full
threescore & ten, but now my numbers tell,
she says, a different story: I am twice
as likely as your average man to fall

victim to my heart. When you factor in
family history, forget it; my ticker
is a time bomb, as if I didn't know.
In matters of the heart, I always go
strictly by the numbers, after all,
counting down to the certain end of the line.

SCORING

Six in the spring, my son's become obsessed
with boundaries overnight & seems determined
to fence himself in with four orange cones
of the kind that form dotted lines on highways
around car accidents, breakdowns, & road
repairs but, in his hands, stake out end zones
on his imaginary Soldier Field

in our backyard. He once thought nothing out
of bounds who now plows across the goal line
in the snow, the ball tucked in his armpit
instead of running with it like a kid
"stealing a watermelon" (my bear-like
father's words teaching me, his little
Bronko Nagurski, how not to hit

pay dirt). I learned my limits at five, too,
standing with Grandpa outside the dime store:
he wouldn't set foot on its snow-squeaky floor
beneath its slow-motion ceiling fans
to buy me a toy car, pleading poverty
despite (in my view) the Northwestern Bank
across the street, & thereby saved the day.

Much as my boy has come to concentrate
his energies by playing games with rules
&, in the fall, will go to school to find
the letters he prints will only spell words
if he toes the fine lines on his ruled paper,
I force myself to live within my means
& count my syllables to make them count.

from SECOND HOME *(2001)*

CHANGE OF LIFE

My friend the player vows he's written off
meaningless sex—i.e., sex without love—
but by a certain age all lovemaking
should be an end in itself, not the means
to somebody's end, with no point beyond
the feeling of two souls conjoined to try
& give each other pleasure without end.

Since cutting to the payoff means letting
the future call the shots, as in the past,
the only way of staying in the present
moment remains to use the rhythm method
& draw out time by putting off the climax,
much as working the ins & outs of syntax
slows my progress toward the bottom line.

FIRST LOVE

I want to see you naked & your face
when you come—that's all I want to see said
about love anymore when desire threatens

it's run its course. Item: your dress made
of silk the green of sea foam & as plush
to the touch as a pink-gold apricot

takes our decades together off my age
each time you wear it, as you must, with nothing
under its latticework of straps in back

& sheath fit with a slit up front. Its side
zipper allows, as now, both my hands easy
access to the sunless globes of your T

& A, which I have brought to light. They feel
exactly as my ten fingers remember.

CAST-IRON BLIMP

Is it related to a lead balloon,
this silver Tootsietoy of heavy metal
fashioned like a zeppelin Collectibles
Unlimited wheels out & floats for upwards
of a song? Anchored by its sky-high price,

it still gives rise to my construing, al-
chemist of memory I aspire to be,
my father's dwelling on the *Hindenburg*'s
going down in flames as his private image
of truth: enterprises fueled by hot air

were fated to crash & burn. My small business
has been not to forget his word was gold
since I went underground & first sat down
at his weighty gilt-lettered Underwood,
holding my breath to see what words would fly.

IN A WORD

Poetry is really a form of worship.
Robert Hayden

Sunday my neighborhood church rang a bell
as if for me, but I turned a deaf ear,
islanded as I was by boxy Stanzas,
Isuzu Styluses, & Mercury
Tracers. Soon my Accord flew me beyond
where the last freeway, like railroad tracks run
into the ground, ran out of gas in weeds.

Landing in the cratered parking lot
of an abandoned dog track, I got down
on my knees before the white elephants
displayed like holy relics at a swap meet
vaster than any rummage sale that Nana
could have imagined mounting in the basement
of St. Olaf's. I retrieved her red-&-white-

handled bread knife she used on loaves she'd baked
with flour stored in the wine-red bin beneath
her apron-white counters, next to the cupboard
where I stashed my green wood-&-cast-iron
flatbed I didn't want to lose when moved
into a new house at seven. My first
brass-buttoned Rawlings glove my dad gave me

for Easter came to light, plus his shotgun
(in its tan leather case) he kept well-oiled
deep in the farthest reaches of his closet,
& even the linen print Grandpa brought
my mom home from Mexico reappeared
out of nowhere, its sombrero'd Rip Van
Winkle there under his saguaro. The world

I'd known back at my feet, I lost track of time
among its findings, but what I found missing
& gone for good was my child's faith in prayer—
unless this mumbling to myself I do,
not from or by the Book but in a book,
amounts to worshiping a greater power
that promises a future for the past.

EMPIRE BUILDER

Trains have carried me away ever since
my mother's mother scolded her (I heard)
in Minneapolis because she stepped
off the Hiawatha from Chicago

pregnant with me, while the Forty-Niner aimed
to ship my just-commissioned father west
of the Golden Gate into the Rising Sun.
Transported by the hoot the Minuteman gives

shooting through Providence again tonight,
I backtrack to the eight-year-old I was,
burning my fingers on the silver rails
nearly molten in the August heat

as I sacrificed my blackest copperhead
to the tanked-up Empire Builder that would pass
below my Golden Valley ranch with cargo,
under wraps, targeted for Korea.

Fifteen years down the line, my hands were tied
the April afternoon I couldn't look
when a green train bursting with greener kids
bound for the jungle screamed through my backyard

outside Richmond. When I left home the fall
before & rode the last Orient Express
from Paris to its end in Istanbul,
I never dreamed I'd starve till past Trieste.

A guest worker escaping Munich wanted
my blue Parker fountain pen for his bread
but didn't know I meant to live by ink,
hungry to swallow the world whole like this.

SECOND HOME

for Mutlu

I

Duty-free Hermes in my pocket now,
your Joy postponed again, Memorial Day
I'm back mixing spirits with Blondie soda.
Each lemon-lettered bottle is the green
of an Astroturf mini soccer field
fenced in on the scorched earth between a mosque
—"*Allah* in Xmas lights!"—& cinder blocks
by law a house if crowned with the trademark
corrugated Eternity-brand roof
against the elements. (Once four in number,
they were themselves the building blocks, as per
local lore.) Meanwhile, Izmir has named
its new airport after a glamour boy
prime minister folks hated to see hanged.

II

Your father's house he bought with precious metal
on his deathbed is history today,
undermined by a high-rise boom & paper
bills all colors. On the five, emerald-cloaked
Rumi yields to the thick-waisted hourglass
of a sepia cooling tower, time changed
from a grain-by-grain trickle to a landslide
& family plots to story upon story.
Even as I write, F-16s crackle
like thunder off the balcony the powers-
that-be dictate the narrow limits of.
The lightning is day breaking on the cart
a turbaned milkman's decked with thumbnail landscapes,
his white nag rainbowed with pom-poms & tassels.

III
Sailing home on the ferry from the Old
Gold Market, I sat beside—his card read—
"Mr. Charly" (*sic*). He asked me point-blank
what it felt like being a citizen
of the country the whole world has in mind,
the way at lunch *USA* was tattooed
in lime & lemon close to the hearts of both
the pizza thrower & his Boy Friday.
My seatmate was a jeweler where we'd come from,
& coincidence refreshed my memory
of how events are riddled with connections,
much as gold was the thread that tied our lives
together, wound around my finger like string
that once returned me constantly to you.

IV
Humming the Marines' hymn still gives me gooseflesh.
My boy won't hear of it but sings a Turkish
anthem about Gallipoli, where one
among my Welsh grandfather's fourteen siblings
(James), shot on horseback in a custom-printed
postcard from the front, fought a losing battle.
Artichokes are bristly thistles whose heads
were meant to roll, I see from someone's field.
Marched to the sea, my son drops his M–16
facsimile near a Greek War redoubt,
his future a question mark; thyme, still green,
goes to my head. I aim to freeze the scene
the way jam preserves in amber the scent
of last summer's peaches, flushed & inflamed.

V
My kid missed his carotid artery
by a hair last night, slipping off a wall
onto a stake that shored up oleanders.
The night before, I'd seen him lying flat
on his back in a dream—dead to the world,
to all appearances—& feared the worst.
I found him hollering, an arrow lodged
deep in his throat, & plunged into the dark
for a medicine man. Going back six years,
the second he was born I saw in him
my father, who nearly stabbed his jugular
when he tripped running downhill with a knife
at six. His mother bore him to a doctor,
who stitched him up. His life hung by a thread.

VI
Green crosses earmark this holiday's victims
huddled like a team of all followers,
putting their heads together to no purpose.
Their flesh haggled over & sold for X
number of pink & orange bills, the shepherds
give them each a last pat on the back,
rope them into car trunks, & slam the lids—
hostages without blindfolds or duct tape.
My black-eyed, -eared, & -nosed white lamb, with patches
of *café-au-lait* & polka-dotted shins,
gets his throat slit in Allah's name tomorrow,
sacrificed so that I can thank the gods
my son survived an accident in his blood,
the nick in his neck Artemis's mark.

VII

The blades the town's itinerant knife-sharpener
honed finely yesterday have done their work.
The thin man hunched over his portable
four-legged stand in the shade kept his nose
to the grindstone he set spinning when he tapped
his right foot, as if marking time to music
he alone heard. Each hysterical victim,
first blindfolded with a white muslin scarf
used to cover a woman's hair in mosques,
was slashed from ear to ear to please a higher
power worshiped by spilling blood for real,
the gauze-like cloth stained red indelibly.
This morning I still feel the heat beneath
the olive where my animal's strung up.

VIII

The butcher takes the head (the brain & tongue
delicacies), the tail for tallow, hooves
for gelatin. The snaky entrails get
unceremoniously buried, nothing
beyond a hole beneath the reach of dogs.
An air-force tractor gathers up the skins
to keep the butts of Phantom fighter pilots
toasty at unfathomable altitudes
when they go dueling with the Greeks' Mirages.
The still-warm flesh lies quivering in pans.
We'll eat the lion's share of meat; the rest
will feed the poor, night-watchmen & their kin,
who sacrifice their days that I may sleep
in peace, dreaming A-bombs on CNN.

IX

All smiles & green eyes, the watchman who fled
the Kurdish bloodbath in the east by running
off with a smuggler's daughter once went out
on someone's limb & shook down mulberries
for me; I came home bloodstained as a butcher.
Then things slowly disappeared from our place:
a single hand towel, a favorite sweater,
an emerald Volvo & a ruby Saab
from our boy's collection of Hot Wheels, a rug.
When the cops tried returning to their rightful
owners some stolen goods found in the cave
where his wife had caught him with her best friend,
the mullahs called our missing rug their mosque's,
but he confessed he'd lifted it from us.

X

A Black Sea village girl of five, your mother
glimpsed herself squished upside down in a round
mirror small as a pocket watch—no doubt
the only looking glass at home—inlaid
below the latch of the hope chest she'd sprawled
across & recollected suddenly,
thanks to the chest I had just bargained for:
green & decorated with Trees of Life
(charcoal branches of pear-shaped saffron flowers).
She'd wondered, she recalled some sixty years
later, if she could crawl inside & find
herself. By opening in memory
that box roughly the size of a child's coffin,
she met the face behind her face at last.

XI

On his red bike my son shows me myself
on mine at the same age, but training wheels
have given him the hand my father lent
to me, going in circles in our yard.
When I finally straightened out, resisting
gravity's pull with my balancing act,
I shot across the lawn toward the street
my mother, raising her head from her nonstop
sewing, reminded me had been dug up.
Unmindful of her last words, I went sailing
off the deep end. I still can't keep my feet
on the ground, driven to such unwitting flights
as this. My son flies down the road, his face
now my mother's bent over her machine.

XII

I tell the watchman at Erythrae we met
seven years ago when, unknown to me,
my son here got a foothold in his mother.
The guy shows me what they have meant for him—
no teeth in half his mouth. The Byzantines,
says the cross of a new TV antenna
springing from his ruin, have the last word.
Green thumbs of almonds, down-turned, nix the Romans.
Artichokes, gone to seed, sprout tufts as purple
as urchins in the sea that brought Greeks from Troy.
Above it all, mock dogfights buzz like static.
Among the shards of earthenware my boy
collects, a snake hacked in two stops me cold:
time, that great leveler, will cut me short.

XIII
In the sanitarium at Pergamum
the S-shaped snakes carved in stone hiss in English.
You thought they looked a little more than phallic
when I spied a postcard of an oil lamp
(Roman) in the museum, which depicted
a man taking a woman from behind.
While he reclined, she obviously writhed,
beside herself, the back of her hand pressed
against her brow. I searched for the pedestals
inscribed to Homer, Sappho, & the guy
who invented parchment. The child I was
discovered it in Philadelphia
in a browning Declaration. The world turns,
it said, on how we represent ourselves.

XIV
Seyyid gives me his word I take him at
that his shop's kilims are as soft as silk,
all natural, & indestructible.
Just as the truth lies somewhere in between
his claims & my suspicions, we arrive
together at the final cost by splitting
the difference between the fortune that he asks
& the pittance I first offer in return.
I feign indifference to the piece I crave;
acting, too, he complains he'll sacrifice
his profit. In the end I pay the price
I can afford, while he gets what he needs.
Such back-&-forth weaves the social fabric.
In fact, "shopping" translates as "give-&-take."

XV

On Sunday yet it fell into my hands,
a Koran handwritten three hundred years
before & sold to me without profit
by Muslim law, which also says it mustn't
ever sink below my bellybutton.
The scribe who copied out its words repeated
the Prophet's deed of taking down God's word
by dictation. Blood-red, a drop of ink
punctuates each couplet. Lulling my will
asleep—losing myself in counting beats
per measure—& submitting to the law
of numbers, I inscribe what comes to mind
out of nowhere, as it seems, much the way
the lines before me now originated.

XVI

Under the Marshall Plan, Kazim the agri-
culturalist uprooted Reds from Rhode
Island, which rule the roost in Turkey now.
As a boy, he learned German from his father,
an officer times made the Kaiser's ally,
then taught himself English & the Persian
I hear when he recites Omar Khayyam.
Cultivating the roots of words, he argues
Allah arises from Egyptian's *ox,*
sacred for the shot in the arm it gave
crops with its droppings when it plowed a furrow.
Its hieroglyph, turned on its head, reads *alpha*
in Greek & *A* in Latin. What he's not
saying, I am: the alphabet is God.

XVII

When I stepped out of Turkey's shipping lines
after booking passage to the Greek island
opposite where Homer was born, the town
fell quiet in the wake of a small craft
built for one that, flat-bottomed, bobbed along
as wave on wave in a sea of hushed men
launched a featherweight upon the waters
via the mosque. The day before, tradition
set the poor soul's worn brogues outside his door
for whoever needed them to cross over
to spring from fall & winter, when the weather
here calls for leather in any shape or form.
Picking up where the dead left off myself,
I still get cold feet filling their black shoes.

XVIII

First, the Greek sister in a habit nodded
across the lake-sized gulf & spat out, "Turkey!"
Then she unveiled the 1822 bones
of the 25,000 Greeks on Chios
memorialized in verses by Lord Byron
—she showed me his handwriting on the wall—
& mourned each Easter there for getting burned
in church by Turks, who'd lost (she failed to mention)
as many Muslims to firebrands from Samos.
I wish that both parties worshiped their common
mother, sea-blue earth, not their different fathers
indifferent in heaven. At the Pearly Gates,
souls give their mothers' names, because they know
for certain only who their mothers are.

XIX
Bias, the first autobiographer,
came from Priene, as did the first woman
architect, Phile, who designed this city's
reservoir that survives in principle
as the spring-fed pool at its watering hole
some drunk tourist is always diving into.
I raise my son to occupy the throne-
like stone seat reserved for whoever climbs
to its theater, no once-in-a-lifetime
ascent to Alexander-proof Termessus
but a trip to the top of the then known world
I've taken four straight decades. In the spirit
of Priene's aptly named native son,
I slant my history toward myself.

XX
You who collect seashells on every beach
gathered them in Miletus, where the sand
that, silting up the harbor over time,
left it high & dry & buried the marble
columns paving the way to Didyma.
Once a year the holy flocked there to pay
Apollo homage & get their fortunes told
by a sacred source. Walking in their shadow,
I knew their future, having read their past,
& shared, if not their faith in a wellspring
of voices, their fate your shells made concrete.
We took the road destined in the end
for oblivion, leaving in our day
Thales Café for Hotel Oracle.

XXI

I'd hardly come to a full stop in Konya
when a guy started pitching me a kilim
& I heard music drifting from a flute.
Rumi's tomb smelled like a gymnasium
from pilgrims marching past in sweaty socks
as if inside a mosque. Lightning jumped
between a bearded merchant & a woman
flashing just her eyes & ankles. Dating
back ten centuries, before the Ottomans
prevailed & outlawed representing humans,
Seljuk ceramics in the dim museum
you dug up there featured your button nose,
thin lips, & coffee eyes wide-set like Jackie's
that bought & sold me all those years ago.

XXII

Evening in Cappadocia. A shepherd
leading his flock to water to the tune
of his flute wore his woolen sports coat
draped over his shoulders à la Marcello
Mastroianni in *La Dolce Vita*.
His lambs drank peacefully from the same stone
oasis of a spring that satisfied
my own thirst not a minute earlier.
I saw the sun burn down to nothing more
than one red coal small as his cigarette
glowing in the night that slowly welled up.
Darkness closed the book on another day,
his sheep folded between plain brown wrappers.
His flute calls the tune of that chapter still.

XXIII

I'd flown to Bird Island when my mother
landed at Izmir's old air-base airport
with no one meeting her & wept alone
on your doorstep, reported neighbors, shaking
their heads at how her son could let the woman
find herself a room in a foreign city.
She never mentioned my snafu.
At heart I couldn't share my reverie
of summer in the holy land I'd found.
Worse, I felt embarrassed when each new sight
only resembled what she'd seen at home.
In twenty years I've come to realize
I follow in her footsteps everywhere,
linking my days with correspondences.

XXIV

Her firebombed temple coin-bright silver pools,
I stand in awe of blissed-out Artemis
of Ephesus again. At first I figured
she was all alabaster breasts, except
they had no nipples, & on second thought
I saw her honeycombed with eggs, unless
this patron saint of virgins wouldn't make
an emblem of fertility. In fact,
she's hung with testes representing bulls
castrated in her honor like the priests
unmanned by their own hands to serve Diana
(as she was later known) or, earlier,
Cybele. Each new initiate of hers
ran howling through the streets & flung his bloody

XXV

organs through an open door at random;
the lucky household owed their former owner
food & clothes for life. No Medusa
freezing me with a look at Didyma,
she shares the Buddha's *Mona Lisa* smile
fixed in marble, as if inviting all
such meanings as she is invested with
—goddess, mother, virgin, slut, & witch.
My mother, Mary, had the wrong idea
about you when she sold you on not buying
a white dress for our wedding but a gold
you could recycle some less august day,
only to show up wearing white herself.
The Virgin Mary lies not far from here.

XXVI

While I sat scribbling in my room as always
the morning of our wedding on this day,
you tangled with the beauty operator
Mary, who'd turned your head into a beehive.
The week before, Helen in your office cried
at Tonkin Gulf, a Cassandra in her way;
torched on-screen, Watts previewed decades. At night
the Beatles, not the Twins, played at the stadium,
& at Cape Kennedy Apollo 5
shot for the moon. When guests showed us the door,
we stepped—half-blind—into the dark future
everyone but us knew would see us hit
earth-shaking thunder & sky-splitting lightning,
found here in August once in a lifetime.

XXVII

There I stood in some astronaut's ex-pad
in the east Eighties, twenty-five stories
closer to the moon than the man on the street,
& talked long-distance to my eighth-grade friend
about our common flame of two decades
ago. Sometimes I still slow-dance cheek to cheek
with her to "Earth Angel" down his basement,
her pointy little breasts under her crimson
sweater tickling my ribs, et cetera,
& I still see him walking out the door
to Enga's Funeral Home with a blue suit
for my father, whom he'd trusted to inform
a scoutmaster had gotten friendly with him
inside a tent. Speaking from Chicago,

XXVIII

where I last saw him over a six-pack
of Falstaff's the night before he moved out
to Vietnam, he couldn't tell his mother
wrote him off behind his back a "confirmed
bachelor" & a "dyed-in-the-wool"—her words—
Republican. His father turned up bombed,
a specialist from Ithaca in feed,
& volunteered the phrase "American
civilization" was a contradiction
in terms. The scene flashed back to me tonight
like a streaking meteor when I sat down
to nose around among the stars & play
connect-the-dots with ancient constellations,
the way I fill in the blanks of the past.

XXIX

Turquoise fades from the sea & sky alike,
the sun paler than a Communion wafer.
A pleasure craft trailing a sprightly caique
scurries to dock before the light dies.
Kids gladly follow home their moms' aroma
of steaming pilaf. A tortoise-shell tom
steals into some corn, waiting for the mice
that will show up at dark. A black goat
steps out of the shadow of an olive.
Flighty little nondescript birds get heard.
A cow lows to be milked, her calf kicking up
his heels. All flesh looks peachy at the last.
Someone fresh from the shower smells like rain.
Lightning in her eyes. Thunder in my heart.

XXX

When I was thirty-something, I risked life
by smoking a bootblack's hash in Istanbul
& almost got greased by a chrome DeSoto,
walking under the influence. Five years
before, convinced a harmless-looking blue
Nova parked across Hope Street had my number,
I'd flushed my stash & switched to vitamins.
I "let it go," in the famous last words
of the Beatles. You had flown the first jumbo
jet here that summer for the operation.
Never again, I vowed, & would remember.
Back home, long hair cropped, you passed me an egg,
an onyx symbol of fertility
I brooded on until you hatched a life.

WISHFUL THINKING

1. Message in a Bottle

I lose the light before it is too late
to see Labor Day's wispy new moon
curve into the ocean, an eyelash blond
as my appleseed-brown-eyed son's eyebrows
bleached by the sun as if caked with dried salt
one last time before he enters first grade
tomorrow. Summer's closed parenthesis,
the crescent moon lighting on the horizon
becomes a white sail bellied out by wind
& rides into the sunset even he
finds unnerving. I want to say to him:
We've all been there; the secret is to make
your way back here, where beach glass is as good
as currency, but able to read this.

2. Rough Draft

Holding his heart & seeing stars, my boy
stands behind bars as red as the fine lines
his class keeps inside to carve out small letters,
feet on the ground, & pledges his allegiance
to the flag without stumbling till he draws
a blank at *under God* (Ike's little add-on
in my day), *indivisible* proves a tongue-
twister, & *justice for all* gives him pause.
Word by brave word, the lump in my throat grows
as I remember coming to attention
every last morning ended with my marching
into school & signing up for the draft
the morning after I had turned eighteen,
putting my life on the line in no time.

3. Autobiography

When you write stories, it's okay to tell
what's happened in your life. My sentiments
exactly, except they're my first-grader son's
reason for not dreaming up aliens
for his illustrated narrative. Drawing
on the granddaddy of an octopus
he saw make short work of a crab last August,
he's represented it as also penning,
with one free arm & in the ink he witnessed
bled from it, a purple crayon likeness
of the blue Magic Marker original
it's eating. He figures life happens twice—
first out there & then in here, where it shows
its true colors once it's captured on paper.

4. S-Curve

The clock in my Honda doesn't let my kid
circle back in time, its numbers composed
of lines straight as the roads that bore him always,
high-waisted jack pines waving on both sides.
Its stoplight-green read-out lacking in curves,
he rages in the back seat, at six partial
(like Navajos rounding off with white blankets
their foursquare red shoulders) to twists & turns,
because his eye apes the pear-shaped blue planet
school has taught him is the apple of it.
Still, I see myself in him when he takes
the long way around again winding down
to the point of his short story, twisting words
& putting his heart in each turn of phrase.

ROCK COUNTRY

(Oxford County, Maine)

Here all the dead outnumber the living,
& what my father called a "marble orchard"
rises around each turn. Centuries past,
his people landed a stone's throw from where,
stop-sign red, my Cardinals cap guards against
far-from-distant shotguns aimed at small birds,
as I dream mother lodes of amethyst
or tourmaline but only strike fool's gold.

I've never looked his headstone in the face
whose rage for hunting had me popping off
in woods like these myself some forty years
ago this fall. I kneel with my own son
in quartz-cold air flecked with snow like mica,
digging for the stone with my name on it.

THE BOYS

Toward the end it got too dark to say
who was who in the father-&-son game
commemorating the last soccer season.
Play no sooner began than the pale sun
of November gave up the ghost, the earth
frozen the earliest in living memory.
By virtue of my age, I stood my ground
in goal, the final line of defense against

the kids. Shadows kicking the shins of shades-
to-be, they swarmed me in the gloom of dusk
& took their shots, my son for a hat trick.
Then time ran out, & with the other boys
he celebrated "killing the old guys."
Hearing about it all the long way home,
I hated thinking that someday we'd go
wordless into our separate nights, like men.

DAYLIGHT SAVING

1

The first bees of the season buzz the snowdrops
hanging their heads & staring at their feet.
My father plants his foot in the springy earth
& throws out the season's first pitch, the ball
white as I remember the first snowfall.
His mitt, a Bill Doak model blackened by dirt
from the Thirties, fits him like a glove; mine's
too big for me. As much a ghost as him
in time, I see myself a memory
in my son's eyes as we play catch this morning
in our backyard, the new hardball his first.

2

I'm standing in my father's shoes, a decade
older than he was when he raked the earth
for my new Little League, my sneakers black
like his Converse high-tops. After forty years
he's golden on the skinned infield the long-
lost sun spotlights, the center of a diamond-
in-the-rough as he fungoes kids would-be
bleeders. Each grounder that he hits kicks up
the dust he'll be in ten years. The clock turned
forward last night, I'm stepping off baselines
five feet at a time for my son's first practice.

COUNTDOWN

As I collect my son from hide-&-seek,
asking him to call it a day & stop

blending with shadows as if going back
to where he hid out before he was born,

I could be standing on a shore & casting
lines into the blue in the hope a form

I know by heart will swim out of the dark
in silence, stealing "home" ahead of "It."

(Who'd choose to hang his head & count to ten
while everyone dissolves into the night?)

I tear my boy from play & march him off
toward the house & sleep—toward the time

that I won't see, I mean, when there will be
no one to find him or to walk him home.

RETRIEVER

"I wish I had a dog to take me different
directions," my boy sighed as he trudged home
from school in his last week of being ten
& watched a headstrong golden drag its human
companion through the mud at the end of her rope.

Everybody is gone who always said
I'd no sooner learned to walk than I vanished
from Nana's picket-fenced backyard washday,
only to be spotted hours later climbing
Ilion tied to the collar of her springer.

When I repeated his words, my son countered
they sounded like a song, as if he knew
he'd handed me a line I'd grab & let
lead me back through memory to retrieve time.

BESIDE THE HOLY CITY'S SACRED POOL

Once at Hierapolis, a booked-up ghost town
of a Roman necropolis with hot springs
where German little Caesars burn in sulfur,
a belly dancer neither young nor old
—castanets snapping like spun roulette wheels—
gyrated up to me all hips & lashes.

Forehead & upper lip sequined with sweat,
she whispered in the current lingua franca
the dirty word *money* & spoke her mind
in body language that said loud & clear,
My left cup runneth over with large bills,
in hopes that I, a tourist trapped, would get
the message I should pad her other breast
with wads of cash. I gave her all I had.

TOWARD AN ANNIVERSARY

Under the sun back at its height in June,
a legless beggar spun round, dervish-wise,
frantic to catch the eye of each passerby
he made sidestep his limp, empty Levi's
twisted in Smyrna's cobble-stoned agora
like Caesar's limbs contorted by a seizure.

Winding up a stairway that turned above
the swarm of streets into a honeycomb
of shops, I found a goldsmith in his cell
—behind locked doors & in the air-conditioned
isolation that glorifies the end
of this particular millennium—

& asked if he who could work miracles
would gild your hand-carved coral cameo
of Aphrodite in her bliss, a gift
commemorating ages spent intact.
Below, my guilt recalled, one still awaited
wild-eyed the miracle of some small change.

WESTERN EXPOSURE

Back on the cliff walk to the Gulf of Chios
for a sunset swim, I fell in behind
three women wrapped from head to toe in patterns
of every color. Dressed as they believed
Allah desired, they felt their time had come,
the topless & all-but-bottomless tourists
gone now, their god brought low at last. Surprised
by me in my Speedo, they retraced their steps
in a hurry. Leaving, though, I passed the spot

where they had moved to get their feet wet, stockings
under shalvars beneath ankle-length skirts.
Two of them turned their backs, but the third lifted
her open face to me as the sun went down.
Smiling, I wished her *Good evening* in Turkish,
& under the gold scarf concealing her hair
like a halo rubbed out at St. Sophia,
she flashed an olive-eyed smile in return,
as if we shared the same day in the sun.

MINOR RUIN

Come summer, I would always stop to worship
at what's left of the temple Teos raised

to Dionysus. It's the way I paid
homage to his devotees, who loved too well

the spirit's blood—wine dark as Homer's sea
beyond the olives—& wowed small towns all

across Ionia with their song & dance.
Except their fellow citizens got sick

of how they acted while at home & banished
the whole gang to a village so remote

it doesn't have a name in history.
But when the Persians rode out of the east,

even the city fathers called it quits,
escaping into exile with the rest.

Abandoned to this day, the spot is best
remembered in the end as the birthplace

of the Greek poet Anacreon, who died
as he had lived by choking on a grape seed.

OUT OF EDEN

For years on end I saw our naked crimson
hibiscuses ("Japanese roses" there)
forever blossom fifty to a bush
in a day but then go limp, shriveled up

to nothing by sunset. Each morning after,
June strawberries you'd melted down to jam
in the sun would ruby my plate drop by drop,
redder than ever after August showed

the dark side of the light. One last summer
slowly bled to death, the way my "heart"
—so called for lack of a better word—withered,
under fire from you during each night's battle.

HOME FROM IONIA

Another summer & its August sex
suddenly in the past, I caught myself

going downhill back in the land of autumn.
A lone copper beech leaf fell at my feet,

its downward spiral echoing the upward
swirl of smoke from my nightly barbecues

of coral fish, black eyes, or Day-Glo orange
deep-water red mullets netted as far

below the Aegean as the smoke got off
the ground before always losing itself

in the Milky Way. Greasing my skids, acorns
oaks scattered like lost marbles in my path

set me up for a fall, but I knew green
olives still clung to my tree as a yellow

jacket with matching kneepads drilled them for oil
my neighbors there would strike, distilling gold

from the sun the way I turn ancient history
here into the elixir of memory.

NEW POEMS *(2005)*

BYZANTINE BIRD

Back in the ruins of Byzantium,
I went to market & explored a stand
that sold canaries, where I stood & watched

a golden songbird with a chartreuse breast
pound his little marmalade-crested head
against the bars of his far-from-gilded cage.

My chest tightened in the open air,
& I got claustrophobic when I saw
how he would beat his black-lined wings as if
the sky were not beyond his reach for good.

Frantic & panic-stricken though he looked,
he launched into a song out of the blue,
his consolation for his pain a joy
to hear. I left him behind bars of music.

THE ALEXANDRIA EXPRESS

The grimy windows of the train from Cairo
rendered the clear March morning overcast

as I sat down & unpacked my cold breakfast
the Hotel Mena had boxed up for me.

My first evening there, I thought clouds loomed
over it, before I saw with a gasp

they were the pyramids gone cinnamon
in the dying light. My first sight of bookish

Cavafy's haunts proved the stonewashed Med,
my nose buried in it, pressed to the glass.

Swarmed by kids in the streets, Arabic Greek
to me, I shot them wildly when they begged,

faceless, to be immortalized on film
as their ramshackle city is on paper.

WHO SHALL REMAIN NAMELESS

"Chips," because so many boys got a piece
of her, not to mention "skag" & "skank" (words

as ugly as her mom found her name lovely),
where did she go who played as fast & loose

with her good name as she was generous
with her new body, charcoal hair & lips

hot pink? I never touched her, though, except
she smiled at me as I felt myself pressed

against her in a crowd, escorting her
around the school when she returned "reformed."

Ahead of her time, she saw us all as dead-
end kids already, & lived like there was no

tomorrow. Backward, I lived for it & learned
too late from her there's no time like the present.

CREATURE FEATURE

In his small way my teen had said good-bye
to childhood by twelve, then a huge collector
of muscle cars & muscle men scaled down
to sizes that he could imagine handling.

Although he'd die to measure up to them
one day, he was incensed Godzilla II
got killed off—a "smart but misunderstood"
victim, in his eyes, not the villain.

Grieving for himself, he'd spent half his life
playing Billy Budd to a bully's Claggart
& acting as the class scapegoat since six.

In the battle of the species at the end,
he didn't root for *Homo sapiens*
but felt for the lizard, having been a kid.

ARRHYTHMIA

Today I exercised my heart by watching
my fifteen-year-old get his second wind
& run the fifteen-hundred under five.
Flying around the track, his red-&-gold
shoes barely touching umber earth, my son
lightened my heart, heavy as it was
with grave matters when I compared our ages.

Four decades between us, I saw him go
in circles through the coming years—head high,
eyes clear, his feet keeping time with his heart.
This year I've lived longer than both my father,
a four-letter man with a fifty chest,
& his before him, my awful heart skipping
a beat every blessed second of my life.

HORROR STORY

I always thought the words *blood-curdling scream*
the stock in trade of cheesy horror stories,
until my teenager curdled my blood

with long minutes of screams his Nokia chanced
to pick up where he lay—I'd learn in time—
beneath his Honda spinning on black ice.

Clutching the phone, I listened helplessly
while my own flesh & blood fought for his life
somewhere at the other end of the line,
wireless as he was. Every parent's nightmare

suddenly real for me, I sat there living
his final moments with him in the dark,
his fearful curses carried through the air
by accident on impact. Then I lost him.

QUILTER

Her Singer with its *thuck-a thuck-a thuck-a*
so zoned me out as it approximated
the tune our hearts play, beating their own drums,

that I returned to Mother's knee, back where
I could discover what would suit me while
she sewed her heart out all the winter day.

Much as my quilter reasoned past her need
for warmth at night when she stitched up her hand-
dyed homespun work of art, my mother sought
to dress in style—not clothe her nakedness—

by fleshing out Vogue patterns. When her mouth
shut on the pins between her lips, I knew
to choose my fabrication: soon the figure
she cut in cloth I'd cut in words on paper.

WHY I DON'T SING KARAOKE

She'd have done it in a heartbeat, my mother
the local radio star & torch singer,
who always warned me carrying a tune

was something I should never try to do
because I'd drop it, even if my life
(she joked) depended on it, each note flat

as a sheet of paper. Like my tone-deaf
father, sentenced to ten years of piano
lessons by his mother, I took a beating

from mine for starting with one song ("Sewanee
River"?) & ending with another ("Rock
of Ages"!) every time. After mangling

"Mack the Knife" on Senior Day, I who'd change
my tune to silence saved my life this way.

PROM NIGHT CONFIDENTIAL

My senior went to his last prom tonight,
& she came back to me, my date to mine,
raped & murdered in a blacked-out alley
behind the Playboy Club in New York City.

She had left work there as a waitress late,
a cocktail Bunny dreaming of Broadway
who had played Blanche in *Streetcar* at the U,
shooting for the stars we Minnesotans

could see each other reach in our inscriptions
on blown-up yearbook photos where we followed
the Method (Palmer) with our Paper Mates.

Spending a lifetime measuring my words
never made me a star, but I'm still here,
whispering in the dark with her offstage.

THE GREAT DIVIDE

There. I've left my freshman holding the bag
between the Rockies & the hard place
where he has found himself on the High Plains,
so far from water it could be the moon.

In view of everybody's distant look,
he's lost among the natives all gold hair
& teeth, laid-back where he is in-your-face,
their voices level as this land of theirs.

His eyes never leaving me as I turned
tail for home in the East in my Yellow Cab,
his thin smile cut like a knife the cord tied

to the now-escaping "It's a boy!" balloon
that signaled his arrival yesterday
but disappears today into the blue.

1963

It was evening all day late that November
when forty-something years ago I came
home for Thanksgiving in the aftermath
of Dallas, back from college like my son
today. I didn't know then that my father
had three months to live, but I learned our neighbor
behind us had gone & gunned his blue Nomad
we borrowed every duck-hunting season
into the path of two teens doing eighty
in a thirty-five zone, killing his blond
daughter, Lynn-Mary, & somebody's baby
a cop said rattled like a bag of ice
when he picked her off Noble Avenue
half a football field down the darkened road.

Outside our picture window, the trees once
turned to gold went as gray as our wood-grain
Zenith, where no one died in living color.
The fall before, in radiant October,
I prayed the world would end with me in heaven
in X, those afternoons when I was golden
because the Cuban missiles were still up
in the air. Now, as usual, my father
shaking like dice the cubes left in his tumbler
signaled my mother that he was fresh out
of Fleischmann's blended whiskey & soft water.
His soon-to-be-stolen Colt .45
held its ground beside his green recliner,
its walnut handle always in arm's reach.

INTELLIGENT DESIGN

My father worshiped God Biology
is all that I remember of the night
I sat at his right hand at our last supper
table. When he saw me for the first time

at two, home from three years of seeing men
shredded like battle flags or blown to nothing
across the South Pacific, he had counted
sacred, he confessed, the fact of my ten

fingers. I count on them as I attempt
to keep the beat I hope will bring alive
this scene a good five decades old. He went

to church, he sighed, to satisfy my mother,
not because he believed in anything
beyond life & its manifold designs.

VISITATION

Living and dying are, in a sense, of equal value.
                    Haruki Murakami

Checking back in this morning with the mirror,
I came face-to-face with my father, gone
some forty years but dressed the way he was

—in a tie & blue jacket—the last time
I saw him from the corner of my eye
where, boxed in, he lay in the funeral home

on Miracle Mile. My mother said he'd joked
they should skip the ER & just stop there
as they bombed by it after his first heart

attack. Three winters later, moments after
his third, he asked her for a glass of water
when the doctors lost him. Not only did

I find him in the mirror resurrected;
I glimpsed at once my present, past, & future.

CANCER CLINIC

That I was booked here on a holiday
before hours says I have no time to lose,
& look, the little estuary painted
& framed to distract patients who await

their fate is missing people. Me, I write
myself out of scene after scene that comes
to mind from all the nights & days I called
my own. A "butterfly" draws blood the double

of every single red that's blessed my life,
especially last night's killed against today
when I'd find out what brought me to this pass.

The doctor practices his laying-on
of hands & speaks in tongues of an "event"
in my red cells. Something is in my blood.

COUNTRY CONVALESCENCE

Paired-off robins surprised in a dust-up
of snow raised my hopes for an end to winter,

but when I dreamed of a green tree with white
blossoms, they changed to snow before my eyes.

Since *health* means *whole,* I had to put myself
back together after falling apart,

& on the day in February when
my father died, I saw the sky at night

float the boat of the crescent moon that crossed
black water with his soul. Still at a loss

for words, I learned that everything coheres
ages ago, thanks to acid. Listen—

birds singing me awake at last? I *wish*:
it's the radiator, letting off steam.

DISCOVERY

My mind in ruins after I dropped acid
the night before, burning up the speed

in it by walking nowhere fast until
daybreak, I carted myself off to Jamestown

in search of the greener pastures friends promised
would be revealed to such a black-&-white

guy as myself. I joined the company
that April ('69) of those who'd come

—& lived (but mostly died) in rooms the stone
foundations that remained proved small as coffins—

to find what they could see, a paradise
that wasn't on the map or even on

the paper I had chewed. I found nothing there
greener than the green of things as they were.

MY EROTIC PLAYGROUP

I couldn't have been more than six when Mimi
from up the block, whose dad flew for Northwest,
asked me to show her mine under the sheet

draped over a card table in my yard
like a towel thrown over a birdcage,
the edges touching the ground all around.

Behind our makeshift four walls, she pulled down
my pants, & I helped her by stretching out
flat on my back, legs stiff, to shake them off,
so that there I stood, reaching for the sky.

Slowly & coolly she sprinkled a handful
of grass over my erection, a child
priestess baptizing me with holy water:
I was on my way, good to go to heaven.

PARTIAL KNOWLEDGE

My boys & I snickered when we got boners
in blond Mrs. Johnson's sixth-grade classroom,
as she moved among our desks & bent over

each work in progress, her breasts nearly tumbling
out of her trademark V-necks cut so low
they proved a gold mine for our eyes. Although

I saw what I could see, I couldn't fathom
grammar, a deep dark mystery to me
of copulas I couldn't penetrate,
pounding my mattress in exasperation,

till I stayed after. Is it any wonder
my life has been unfolding sentences
that take their time but point me where I am
driven, to this day, by my desire?

AFTER ARCHILOCHOS

Hard-charging, all-or-nothing heart,
I know a girl lives among us
who can't take her wide eyes off you—

a lovely, tender bud
of a girl now breaking into blossom
you frighten & make blush.

"Daughter of Amphimedo," I began,
"the best of women the rich earth embraces,
the goddess offers men so many pleasures

besides, you know, the sacred act. Let's kick
back together—just you, me, & the gods—
& speak of things unspoken till it's dark.

Don't be afraid: I won't do anything
but what your heart desires, & I won't venture
any farther than your garden gate."

Having said that, I took her by the hand
& laid her where a thousand flowers bloomed,
first slipping under her my soft wool cloak.

I slid an arm under her neck,
cradling her head to calm her fears,
& felt her tremble like a fawn.

I lightly grazed her hot breasts with my fingers,
& when my feathery touch found her spread-eagled,
I went bone to bone with her naked pubis.

Caressing inch by inch her loveliness,
I was stroking her hair when suddenly
I shot my hot white come all over her.

AFTER SAPPHO

He is a god among us, sitting there
with you & hanging on your every word.
All smiles & rapt attention, he delights
in your honeyed voice,

enchanted by your laugh that makes
my nipples tingle & my heart go wild.
One look at you says it all
& leaves me speechless.

My tongue dries up in my parched mouth.
A grass fire smolders under my skin.
My eyes stop seeing, & my ears just hear
blood drummed into them.

A cold sweat breaks out the length of my body.
I shiver, green grass fanned
into flames by a wind
that burns me alive.

BLOOMSBURY SUMMER

We must love one another or die.
W. H. Auden

How many times I wound my way back home
from Russell Square with her who, gone commando,
would flash me on the Underground's Blue Line,
but now a godless train believers doomed

to their inferno burns where at each break
of day & every midnight the earth moved
under us in bed, the Tube shooting
below our rented garden studio.

When I refused to play rough, she blew up
in my face one night: her fists called for cops,
& if I'd played, they would have thrown the book

at me. Black-eyed but free to go, I lived—
unlike those souls dead-ended at my stop
for what, five summers past, I took was love.

ALL-INCLUSIVE

He knew all the constellations. He had seen them
rise in darkness over heartbreaking coasts.
                                        James Salter

Leaving still-light Boston for darkest Munich,
a station on my way to Istanbul,
I watched the sun rise at midnight my time,
mere hours after it set in the same colors
but in reverse—ending, not beginning,

with black. I caught up with the day, the air
ablaze, beside the Aegean, too bright
to see this afternoon, as I had found it
four decades back when, an American
in the left's line of fire, I kept my English

under wraps on the street. After dark now,
I dodge the spot where TV showed the righteous
blew my fellow tourists sky-high last week
& made them pay for flying to this coast.

BALKAN WIND BEACH

in memoriam Ramo

He christened me a "dirty old man" once
for girl-watching while he told his Cold War
story—just off the boat from Montenegro,
he learned English in bed from what's-her-name,
a "free" American who typed for NATO—
but when his painter's eye checked out the landscape,
what looked to me one color showed him many
shades of light I likened to those of meaning.

Now he's a shade, a shadow on that shore
I've likewise lost for good, as dead to me
as he is to the world. Yet here we stand
in black & white, this dashed-off pen-&-ink,
brothers under the sun as we were then
when we stood there—happy, for all we knew.